THE BERRY COOK-BOOK

Carol Katz

BUTTERICK PUBLISHING

Permission to reprint from the following is gratefully acknowledged:

Stalking the Good Life by Euell Gibbons, published by David McKay Company, Inc., New York.

"Blueberries" from *The Poetry of Robert Frost*, edited by Edward Connery Lathem. Copyright 1930, 1939, © 1969 by Holt, Rinehart and Winston. Copyright © 1958 by Robert Frost. Copyright © 1967 by Lesley Frost Ballantine. Reprinted by permission of Holt, Rinehard and Winston, publishers.

The 500 Hats of Bartholomew Cubbins by Dr. Seuss by permission of the publisher, Vanguard Press, Inc. Copyright ©1938. Copyright renewed 1965 by Dr. Seuss.

"Elfin Berries" from *Poems* by Rachel Field (copyright 1926 by Macmillan Publishing Company, Inc., renewed 1954 by Arthur S. Pederson).

"Elderberry Wine" by Bernie Taupin, published by Dick James Music, Inc.

"The Copper Kettle," words and music by Albert F. Beddoe, © 1953, 1961, and 1964 by Melody Trails, Inc., New York.

"Berries" by Walter de la Mare by permission of The Literary Trustees of Walter de la Mare and The Society of Authors as their representative.

"Strawberries" by Edwin Morgan, published by the Edinburgh University Press of Edinburgh, Scotland.

Design by Dennis Grastorf
Illustrations by Judith Fast
Composition by World Composition Services, Inc.
Pictured on the front cover: Berried Treasure, page 46.

Library of Congress Cataloging in Publication Data

Katz, Carol G.
The Berry Cookbook.

Includes index.
1. Cookery (Berries) 2. Cookery (Fruit) I. Title.
TX813.B4K37 641.6'47 80-10496
ISBN 0-88421-072-3

708 Third Avenue
New York, New York 10017

A Division of American Can Company

CONTENTS

"Berries, eh? There's good cheer when there's berries."
—From a Charles Dickens
Christmas tale, "The Haunted Man"

To Gene, David, and Paul

ACKNOWLEDGMENTS

The Berry Cookbook would not have been possible without the able and friendly help of many people. I wish to thank Irene Goodman, my agent, whose energy and hard work did much to propel this book into being. I am also grateful to my editor, Linnea Leedham, who had the foresight to envision a book on berries even before it was begun, and whose patience, encouragement, and fine eye for detail are integral to every page herein.

Ellen Elliott Weatherbee of the University of Michigan Botanical Gardens generously shared her knowledge of wild berries with me, and Marion Prince of the Washtenaw County Cooperative Extension Service offered both her time and her expertise in the field of home economics. I was also fortunate to have the fine assistance of Jan Longone and the resources of her Wine and Food Library, one of the largest of its kind in the world, as well as the ready and efficient services of the staff of the Ann Arbor Public Library. The Ocean Spray Company provided me with an unexpected gift of cranberries in August, which considerably facilitated the progress of this book.

More assistance with recipes, recipe testing and tasting, and valuable information came from the following people: Jim Anderson; Tilda Bekran; Bertie Bonnell; Martha Ann Crawford; Marilyn Dean; Celia, Hyman, and Saralee Goodman; Cindy Henes; Mary Kalmes; Ida and J. Leon Katz; David and Paul Katz; Anne Kellogg; Leonard Kreeger; Corky Lincoln; Fred Melendez; Kathy Porter; Mary Rowley; Suzanne Royle; Syd Stegman; Erna Schultz; Vicky Schwager; Tommie Watsell; Violet Wycoff; and Anne Yaros.

I especially wish to thank Margaret Shere and Anne Rueter for generously offering their time, support, and creative cooking abilities. And to my husband, Gene, who has probably tasted more berry creations than anyone on earth with both grace and good will, I extend my appreciation and love.

ABOUT THE BERRY COOKBOOK

The Berry Cookbook has been conceived and written for people who wish to make the most of the fruits that grow in delicious abundance off country roads not very far from their homes or that are easily available through quick trips to the supermarket or produce store. Most everyone is aware, for example, that blueberries can be used for muffins and pies, but how many have even imagined the intriguing variety of ways they may be enjoyed—in fresh fruit salads, as a cold soup topped with a dollop of yogurt for a midsummer luncheon treat, or in a red, white, and blueberry creation to give extra festivity to a Fourth of July celebration. Berries may be eaten in a multitude of ways that can only enhance our knowledge of the culinary arts and considerably heighten our pleasure at the table!

It was also my purpose to pay tribute to the many varieties of berries that grow in both wild and cultivated form throughout the United States. To pick or to prepare berries for eating is, in a very real sense, a kind of celebration of the season. A dish of ripe, shining blackberrries served with cream is a way of sinking our teeth into some of summer's sweetness, and the feast of Thanksgiving would be strangely empty without the cranberry, that zesty red morsel harvested in late autumn.

This collection brings berry recipes conveniently together. If you find yourself blessed with several cartons of tempting strawberries in late spring, for example, you can simply turn to this book's chapter on strawberries for a wide selection of the ways they can be prepared, eliminating the need to make lengthy and possibly frustrating searches through many cookbooks.

Many berries can be used interchangeably for the same recipe. Cheesecake, for example, may be topped with blackberries, blueberries, mulberries, raspberries, or strawberries. In this case, the entire recipe is given just once, in the strawberry section, with a brief note as to the other berries that may be substituted.

Every year nature showers upon us a veritable treasure of berries. Be they black, green, purple, or scarlet, they are the jewels of the season, as nutritiously good to eat as they are delightful to see. It is little wonder, then, that berries have prompted poets and writers throughout the years to embark on small flights of fancy. I have seen fit to include their words on these pages, too, as testimonials to the ways that berries can stir the imagination and stimulate a love of whimsy.

Folklore and history also play inevitable roles in this book. Berries have been enjoyed for so many centuries and in so many places that their uses can tell us a great deal about the people who have prepared them. The sheer variety of recipes reveals much about human ingenuity and imagination, and offers as well a quick overview of international cuisines and new insight into ways that the world's cooks—both humble and renowned—have responded to the fruits of their earth.

Down at the Berry Patch

Picking berries yourself is one of summertime's sweetest and simplest pleasures. That strawberry jam you spread on your toast during a wintry November brunch will rosily remind you of the sun-filled June morning you spent plucking the fruit from its branches. It will taste fresher, too, than anything you could have purchased from a supermarket.

Your willingness to pick berries will also reward you economically. The yield of wild berry patches can be had free for the taking, and commercially grown berries are available to pickers for often half the price of those which find their way to retailers.

One of the joys of berry picking is that almost anyone can do it. All it requires is a desire to be out under the sun and the ability to work for an hour or two under leisurely and pleasant conditions. Children often make enthusiastic berriers, and so do their grandparents. Picking berries is, in fact, a truly multigenerational activity.

If you're a city dweller surrounded by concrete and traffic, you may very well shrug your shoulders at the thought of locating a local berry patch. But the food section of your newspaper can probably direct you to a number of nearby farms that welcome urban visitors to their fields. My town's newspaper regularly lists seasonal crops of fruits and vegetables ready for picking. In June the availability of strawberries is announced; in July readers learn about the bounty of currants, gooseberries, and raspberries; and so on through the end of the season, when raspberries make their second and final appearance.

Wear comfortable, loose-fitting clothing when you embark on a berry hunt, because you'll probably have to stoop down to get at those juicy morsels growing low on their branches. Long pants and a long-sleeved shirt make appropriate gear for protecting you from flies and mosquitoes. Cover your feet with sturdy shoes, canvas if possible, because the ground may be wet. Socks are a good idea, too, because if your ankles are bare the mosquitoes will be the first to know. It helps, too, to spray yourself with insect repellant.

Many berry farms have their own containers, but they often charge for them. Bring your own along, if possible. I find that a deep basket with a sturdy handle makes a reliable berry holder. Many people prefer pails or buckets.

Once you are under the sun, you'll find that berry picking has a curiously refreshing effect on your mind. It requires just enough concentration so that conversation usually stops, but not enough to absorb all your thoughts. Whatever worries you may have brought with you will begin to bob about lazily in your head and then disappear. Occasionally, you'll stop your work long enough to admire a bird that darts by or a shy chipmunk scurrying back home. The firmness of the fruit will feel good in your hands, and soon your movements will take on an easy rhythm. And when you leave for the day you'll have not only a basketful of berries but a rested mind and some sun-drenched memories as well.

Wild berrying is a little more rugged than setting out on cultivated fields where the bushes are lined in neat rows. The wild berry picker must often struggle through thickets and areas of dense growth to get at the fruit he desires. Be sure when you embark on an adventure of this kind that your dress is properly protective and the berries you take are edible varieties, such as those described in this book. There are hundreds of berries in the wild, and some of them are poisonous.

Berries Over the Counter

The quickest way to obtain berries is to buy them at the store. Supermarkets are handy for such common items as strawberries (available throughout most of the year from California), and blueberries and cranberries in season. But the less hardy and more unusual varieties like currants and gooseberries rarely see the inside of a supermarket. To buy them you'll have to seek a good produce store that specializes in fresh fruits. Many of these advertise in local newspapers, and the berries they offer will be far fresher than those you will find in the supermarket.

Farmers' markets, of course, feature the very finest fruits you can buy. Most medium-sized towns and cities have their own farmers' markets, which offer breathtaking spectacles of choice produce on a regular basis.

And many of the sellers will be happy to assist you in whatever unusual berry requests you may have.

One of the pleasantest encounters I've had at my local farmers' market involved a search for elderberries. After stopping at stand after stand, I found that none of these rare berries were being sold. But one of the farmers mentioned that they grew on his land and that he would be glad to pick them for me. I ordered two quarts from him, and returned a few days later to find them waiting for me—four cartons at the unbeatable price of two dollars. And I even came away with an elderberry recipe in the bargain!

Cold Facts on Refrigerating Berries

Once you have brought your berries home with you, you'll have to decide quickly how you wish to use them. Place them in covered containers in the refrigerator if you plan to use them within a few days. But remember that most of them, with the exception of blueberries and cranberries, are highly perishable and will not refrigerate well for long periods of time.

Sort them carefully, removing those that are mushy, moldy, or discolored. Remove all twigs and stems before preparing them. Then place them in a colander, rinse gently in cold water, and let them drain. They will then be ready for the recipes given in this book.

Berries and the Deep Freeze

Freezing is the best way to preserve the fresh taste of your berries for any length of time. Happily, they adapt very well to life in the freezer and can be stored satisfactorily for as long as 12 months.

It is not necessary to rinse berries before putting them in the freezer. As a matter of fact, I have discovered that this tends to make them mushy. Washing can be done shortly before you are ready to prepare them for eating. Simply pack them in moisture- and vapor-proof plastic bags or wrap, freezer wrap, or freezer containers. Allow ½ inch of headspace at the top of your containers because fruit expands somewhat during freezing and can force off tops and lids. If you have the space, first place the berries in a single layer on long, shallow cookie sheets and cover them well. Freeze them until they are hard and then put them in deep containers. This method is the best way to maintain firmness and crispness.

Make sure your freezer maintains a temperature of 0°F. Many refrigerator freezing compartments do not, especially the types that have no separate outside door. If your ice cream remains brick solid, your freezer probably maintains a low enough temperature. Berries properly wrapped and stored at 0°F will maintain a good taste and texture and will have most of the nutrients they possessed when fresh off the vine.

Berries Dried

You may prefer to prolong the life of your berries by drying them. This simple, time-honored method will not only preserve their nutritional value, but will save you space as well. Since dried foods lose up to ⅓ of their bulk, two quarts of fresh berries can shrink to as little as 2⅔ cups, an amount you can conveniently store in plastic bags which require little space and are totable enough to be carried along on camping trips. It's no wonder, then, that drying has enjoyed such a revival in popularity!

Dry only those berries that have hard skins. Of those in this book, blueberries, cranberries, currants, elderberries, and juniper berries adapt best to drying. The others dry poorly; strawberries, especially, lose both their shape and color (as they do in baking).

For drying, select ripe berries without blemishes or imperfections. Pierce their skins by plunging them into boiling water for 15 to 30 seconds; then place them in cold water. Drain them well. Place them in shallow wooden drying trays which have been covered by two layers of cheesecloth (the cheesecloth will absorb their juices). Put them in a 120°F oven for an hour and then increase the temperature to 140° for about four hours. The exact length of time will depend on the initial juiciness of the berries. They will begin to rattle on the trays just before they are thoroughly dried, and you will know that they have reached a satisfactory drying point when no moisture can be squeezed from them. Store your dried berries in airtight containers in a cool dark place. Covered glass bottles may be used, or you can select sealable plastic bags. Remember to carefully label your packages.

Berries may be eaten in their dried form as nutritious snacks. They can also be revived and used in recipes that call for baking or cooking. To reconstitute your dried berries, drop them into boiling water, reduce the heat, and simmer until the berries are tender (about twenty minutes). After being rejuvenated, they will increase in volume. One cup of dried berries, for example, will expand to one and a half cups.

Berries Preserved

Berry preserves are loved the world over. Although they may vary in texture and consistency, all preserves are made by cooking fruit with sugar to prevent decay and fermentation. Jam is made with crushed fruit, while jelly is made from fruit juices and maintains a stiffer consistency than jam. Marmalade is jelly with fruit (usually citrus) suspended in it. Conserves (sometimes referred to as "preserves") are prepared like jam, except they often contain several fruits and a variety of extras such as nuts and raisins. All berry preserves, made and labeled in your own kitchen, make welcome and personalized gifts.

All preserves depend on the acidity of fruits, the presence of natural or artificial pectin (a substance that permits jelling), and the addition of large amounts of sugar, which adds sweetness and helps to keep out bacteria.

To preserve fruit successfully, make sure you have the following:

- a flat-bottomed, 8- to 10-quart enameled or stainless steel kettle, with no cracks or chips inside.
- a colander
- canning jars and metal lids without cracks, chips, or rust
- paraffin
- a small double boiler
- a large metal spoon
- a potato masher
- a jelly bag or several layers of cheesecloth
- a timer
- several stainless steel or glass bowls
- a water bath canner
- tongs

Making Jelly

You should begin by sterilizing your jars. First wash them with soap in hot water and rinse well. Then place the jars in a large pot or bath canner, cover them with cold water, and boil the water for 10 minutes. Follow the manufacturer's directions for sterilizing the rims and lids since the procedure varies according to the particular brand used. Keep both jars and seals in hot water until you are ready to use them or they might break when the hot fruit mixture is added.

Prepare the berries as directed, remembering to carefully discard all imperfect specimens, such as those that are discolored or moldy.

You'll probably find that a jelly bag is most convenient in straining juice for jelly, although several layers of cheesecloth draped over a colander will work, too. Jelly bags are sold commercially or you can easily make your own. Make sure that a large glass or stainless steel bowl has been placed underneath to adequately catch all the juice. Remember that the clearest jelly is made from juice that has not been squeezed or wrung from the jelly bag. You'll have the best results if you let the juice flow on its own; this should take no more than 10 minutes from the first to the last drip. Jelly bags or cheesecloth draped over a colander may also be used for juice extraction in recipes calling for soups and beverages.

It is crucial, in making jelly without artificial pectin, to know when the liquid has reached the jellying point. Three simple tests can be used for this purpose:

1. Take the temperature of the boiling water before you begin. Water will boil at 212°F at sea level, and at lower temperatures in high altitude areas. The jellying point will be reached when the liquid reaches a temperature of 8°F higher than the boiling water.
2. Place ½ teaspoon of the boiled jelly on a cold plate and place it in the freezer for 2 minutes. Your jelly is done if the mixture congeals.
3. Dip a cool metal teaspoon into the hot mixture and hold it away from the steam above the pot. Turn the syrup so the mixture runs off the spoon. If it does so in a "sheet" rather than in drops, you'll know that it is done.

You may use metal lids and bands for sealing jelly or you may use paraffin, a wax recommended as a seal for jelly only. When using paraffin, melt it in the top of a double boiler. Fill the hot jars with the fruit mixture to within ¼ inch of the top. Cover immediately with ⅛ inch of the melted wax. Rotate the jars in a "round the world" motion so that the paraffin covers the top completely, making an airtight seal.

Making Jams, Conserves, and Marmalade

Sterilize your jars, bands, and lids as you would for jellies. Prepare the jam or conserve as directed in the recipe, remembering to discard all imperfect berries. Jars, lids, and bands should be hot when the fruit mixture is added. Fill them to ⅛ inch of the top, wipe the rim of the jar to remove any fruit mixture, place the metal lid on top, and screw the band firmly in place. Paraffin should not be used as a seal for jams and conserves as it may loosen.

Many authorities now recommend that jams and conserves be processed in a hot water bath for 10 minutes if they are prepared in a hot, humid climate. This acts as a safeguard against the formation of bacteria. To process them, follow the directions on page 12 for the boiling water bath method, but boil gently for only 10 minutes rather than the 15-minute period required for chutneys. Remove the jars immediately with tongs, then set them upright, several inches apart, on folded towels or wire racks. They should be cooled in this position for 12 to 24 hours.

Remove the bands and tip the jars sideways to check for airtight seals. The seal is tight if no leakage occurs. If the seal is not tight, the jars can be reprocessed within 24 hours.

Bottling Berry Chutneys

Chutneys, made with fruits, vinegars, and spices, are members of the pickle family and add surprisingly tart and tasty touches to your main courses. I must confess that before undertaking this book I had never enjoyed berry chutneys, but now that I've learned to I continue to bring them to the table, where they add a distinctive flavor to meats and poultries.

You can keep chutneys in the refrigerator if you plan to use them quickly, but they must be bottled if you wish to store them at room temperature. Successful bottling requires approximately the same equipment called for in making preserves.

Begin by sterilizing the jars, bands, and lids as you would for jellies. Keep both jars and seals in hot water until you are ready to add the hot fruit.

Prepare the fruit as directed in your recipe and fill the jars with the mixture, leaving ½ inch of headspace. Wipe the rim of the jars with a clean, hot cloth. Place the lid on the jar and tightly screw on the metal band. Even though the band is tight, there will be enough play in the lid to allow air to escape during processing in a water bath. This creates a vacuum that will draw the lid down to form an airtight seal. Do not tighten the screw band further after processing.

Chutneys require a boiling water bath that prevents their being destroyed by bacteria. Preserves, on the other hand, except those prepared in hot, humid climates, are protected against this threat due to their large amounts of sugar. Immerse the filled, sealed jars in actively boiling water in your water-bath canner. The water should cover the jar tops by an inch or two. Cover the container with a close-fitting lid and bring the water back to boiling. Starting to count the actual processing time when the water returns to a boil, continue to boil gently for 15 minutes. Remove the jars immediately with tongs and set them upright, several inches apart, on folded towels or wire racks. Let them cool in this position for 12 to 24 hours.

Be sure to check the jars for airtight seals after very carefully removing the bands. Tip them over sideways: if no leakage occurs, the seal is tight. If it is not, the jars must be reprocessed within 24 hours.

BLACK-BERRIES

A summer without picking wild blackberries would seem like a year wasted.

—EUELL GIBBONS

Blackberries grow in wild abandon throughout nearly all parts of the country. In fact, Euell Gibbons, berry picker extraordinaire, found them growing even in Hawaii! Blackberry cultivation does occur heavily in such northwestern states as Oregon and Washington, but if you seek an experience in wild berry picking, you are likely to encounter the blackberry, since so many of them appear in unmapped and untended berry patches. You'll be glad you did, for they are juicy morsels when popped fresh into your mouth, and they are wonderful for use in the kitchen, where they can be converted into a number of good dishes. Treat them tenderly; they, like the raspberry, are very delicate and easily crushed.

Black and glistening when fresh, they exude a magenta-toned juice that, if combined with cream and other ingredients, produces some intriguing variations of color. Blackberry pie is as rich and deep in color as red wine, while blackberry fool takes on streaks of pastel that are somewhere between being truly pink and truly lavender.

Dewberries, which grow on trailing vines rather than on upright stalks like the blackberry, are actually first cousins to the blackberry and may be prepared in the same ways. Other close relatives are loganberries, boysenberries, and cloudberries, a little-known species that actually grows in the Arctic Circle and the iciest regions of Russia. If you encounter any of these varieties, you may prepare them as you do blackberries. Mulberries, too, are similar to blackberries. To learn more about them, see pages 117–124.

To freeze fresh blackberries, see the general instructions on pages 8 and 9.

Yes, you can buy blackberries both canned and frozen in your supermarket, just in case you are not able to visit your local blackberry patch.

One 16-ounce package frozen blackberries = 1 pint (2 cups) fresh blackberries

One 16-ounce can = 1 pint (2 cups) fresh blackberries

You may use canned or frozen blackberries for the following recipes, but fresh ones, of course, are best.

BLACKBERRY SOUP

Berry soups are often served in Slavic and Scandinavian countries. Accompanied by rolls or fresh bread they make a good, light luncheon on a hot day, or they can be served as a refreshing first course to a dinner.

1 pint blackberries
1 tablespoon lemon juice
2 cups water
3 inches stick cinnamon
⅓ cup granulated sugar, or more to taste
2 cups plain yogurt or sour cream

1. Combine the berries, lemon juice, water, cinnamon, and sugar in a saucepan and bring to a boil. Cover the mixture, and let it simmer until the berries are quite tender, about 10 minutes. Remove the cinnamon stick.
2. Drain the berries, reserving the juice, then sieve them to remove their seeds. Add the berry pulp to the juice and stir in the yogurt or sour cream.
3. Serve chilled.

Serves 6.

NUT DUMPLINGS

1 cup all-purpose flour
2 teaspoons baking powder
1 teaspoon granulated sugar
1 egg
Milk
⅓ cup chopped nuts
1 teaspoon ground cinnamon

1. Sift the flour, baking powder, and sugar into a bowl. Break the egg into a 1-cup measure, mix it well, and add sufficient milk to it to make ½ cup. Add the liquid to the flour mixture and stir to mix well.
2. Add the nuts and cinnamon and form into balls the size of a teaspoon. (It helps to keep your hands moistened with cold water in order to do this.)
3. Add to the blackberry soup just as it begins to simmer (step 1). Or cook dumplings in simmering water for 10 minutes and add them to the soup later. Turn once.

Makes 12 plump dumplings.

MINTED BLACKBERRY-PEACH SOUP

A soup so elegant it may be served as a delightful and unexpected dessert.

3 cups cider
1 teaspoon grated fresh ginger
1 pint blackberries
1 cup dry red wine
1½ tablespoons ground cinnamon
4 peaches of nectarines, sliced thin
1 tablespoon dried mint or 3 tablespoons chopped fresh mint
1 lemon, sliced thin

1. Combine the cider and ginger.
2. Puree 1 cup of berries and 1 cup of cider through a sieve.
3. Return the puree to the remaining cider and berries. Add the wine, cinnamon, and peaches and stir well. Chill.
4. Serve with mint and floating lemon slices.

Serves 4.

BLACK AND ORANGE SALAD

½ cup blackberries
1 cup mandarin oranges
1 cup unpeeled, diced tart apples (about blackberry size)
1½ teaspoons lemon juice
Orange-Yogurt Dressing (page 17)

1. Combine fruits and sprinkle them with the lemon juice. Chill.
2. When ready to serve, put the fruit mixture in 4 small bowls and pass the dressing separately.

Serves 4.

ORANGE-YOGURT DRESSING

2 tablespoons orange juice
⅓ cup mayonnaise
¼ cup plain yogurt
1 tablespoon honey
¼ teaspoon ground ginger
1 tablespoon grated orange peel

1. Combine all the ingredients and chill.
2. Pass at table separately, to be drizzled on fruit salad.

Makes about 1¼ cups.

BLACKBERRY ROSE CREAM

You'll probably have to visit a specialty store to obtain the rosewater. The trip will be well worth it, though, because the rosewater adds beguiling fragrance and flavor to this frothy dish.

1 cup boiling water
One 3-ounce package blackberry gelatin
1 cup cold water
1 cup blackberries
1 cup miniature marshmallows
2 teaspoons rosewater
½ cup heavy cream, whipped

1. Add the boiling water to the gelatin. Stir well to dissolve and add the cold water. Chill until partially thickened.
2. Add the blackberries, marshmallows, and rosewater to the gelatin. Fold in the whipped cream.
3. Pour into a 4-cup mold and chill until set.
4. Unmold to serve.

Serves 4 to 6.

BLACKBERRY CLAFOUTI

A clafouti or "flan" is a simple French peasant dessert in which berries or other fruit are baked in a rich, pancake-like batter. Easy and juicy, with a country taste.

3 eggs
1 cup all-purpose flour
⅓ cup granulated sugar
1 cup boiling milk
2 to 3 cups blackberries
Confectioners' sugar

1. Stir the eggs, one by one, into the flour. Add the sugar and boiling milk and combine well, removing all lumps. Let stand for 2 hours to settle.
2. Preheat the oven to 325°F. Butter an 8-inch baking dish.
3. Pour ¼ cup of the batter into the prepared baking dish. Heat on top of the stove until the mixture begins to set a little. Pour the berries over and sprinkle the remaining batter on top.
4. Bake in the preheated oven for 30 minutes, or until lightly browned and "puffed" on top. (You can do this while you're eating dinner.)
5. Sprinkle with confectioners' sugar, and cut into pie-shaped wedges or squares, and serve warm.

Serves 4 to 6.

BLACKBERRY APPLE BETTY

1 cup all-purpose flour
¾ cup plus ½ teaspoon granulated sugar
1 teaspoon baking powder
½ teaspoon salt
1 egg
1 pint blackberries
3 cups peeled and sliced *tart* apples
2 tablespoons brown sugar
⅓ cup (5⅓ tablespoons) melted butter or margarine
½ teaspoon ground cinnamon
¼ teaspoon ground cloves

1. Preheat the oven to 375°F.
2. Combine the flour, ¾ cup sugar, baking powder, salt, and egg in a bowl and toss with a fork until the mixture is crumbly. Set aside.
3. Put the blackberries and sliced apple into a greased baking dish. Sprinkle with the brown sugar, then with the flour mixture to make a topping.
4. Pour the melted butter or margarine over the topping. Combine the cinnamon, ½ teaspoon sugar, and cloves and sprinkle this mixture over the melted butter.
5. Bake in the preheated oven for 30 minutes, or until the topping is as brown as you like it to be.
6. Serve warm, with cream.

Serves 6 to 8.

PASTRY FOR A TWO-CRUST PIE

2 cups all purpose flour
2 heaping teaspoons sugar
⅔ cup plus 2 tablespoons butter or margarine
¼ cup cold orange juice
Ground cinnamon

1. Combine the flour and sugar, then add the butter or margarine to the flour mixture in small pieces. Blend the mixture with a pastry blender or two knives until it resembles coarse meal.
2. Sprinkle the cold orange juice evenly over the flour mixture and toss with a fork, then form into a cohesive ball, using your hands and working quickly.
3. When the mixture has been patted into a large ball, divide it in half. Roll half of the pastry out and place it in a pie plate; sprinkle with cinnamon and fill with the berry mixture of your choice.
4. Top with the remaining pastry. Bring the edges of both crusts together and flute to form a decorative edge. Cover the edge with a 1½-inch strip of aluminum foil to prevent excessive browning.
5. Prick the top crust all over with a fork (or slash in the center several times) and bake according to the directions in your particular recipe.

Makes enough pastry for an 8- or 9-inch two-crust pie.

TART SHELLS

1. Preheat the oven to 425°F.
2. Make the Pastry for a Two-Crust Pie as directed above.
3. Divide the dough into 8 equal parts and roll each portion into a 4-inch circle. Fit the pastry rounds over the backs of muffin cups, pleating them to fit closely. Prick them all over with a fork.
4. Place the inverted, pastry-covered muffin tins on a large, ungreased baking sheet and bake at 475°F for 8 to 10 minutes. Let them cool before removing them from the muffin forms.

Makes 8 tart shells.

OLD-FASHIONED BLACKBERRY PIE

½ to 1 cup granulated sugar (the amount will depend on whether you use fresh, canned, or frozen berries)
⅓ cup all-purpose flour
1 teaspoon ground cinnamon
1 teaspoon freshly grated nutmeg
1 teaspoon lemon juice
1 quart blackberries
Pastry for a Two-Crust Pie (page 20)
1½ tablespoons butter

1. Preheat the oven to 425°F.
2. Mix the sugar, flour, spices, and lemon juice and stir into the berries.
3. Prepare the pastry, then cut in two pieces and roll out one for the bottom crust; fit into a 9-inch pie pan. Pour the berry mixture into the pie shell and dot with the butter.
4. Roll out the remaining dough and cover the pie with it. (Or make a lattice top by cutting 10 to 12 strips from rolled-out pastry dough; place 5 to 7 strips over pie, then place remaining strips over them at right angles, folding back alternate strips as each strip is added for a woven effect.) Seal and flute the edges and cut slits in the center if you are using a whole top crust. Cover the edges of the crust with a 1½-inch strip of aluminum foil to prevent overbrowning.
5. Bake in the preheated oven for 35 to 40 minutes, or until the crust is golden brown and the juice begins to bubble through.

Serves 8.

BLACKBERRY PINEAPPLE TURNOVERS

Sour Cream Pastry

3 cups sifted all-purpose flour
2 tablespoons granulated sugar
1 cup (2 sticks) butter or margarine
1 cup sour cream

Blackberry-Pineapple Filling

One 8-ounce can crushed pineapple, with juice
1 tablespoon cornstarch
2 tablespoons granulated sugar
Dash each of freshly grated nutmeg and ground cloves
½ teaspoon ground cinnamon
1 pint blackberries

1. Combine the flour and sugar. Cut in the butter or margarine with a pastry blender or two knives until the mixture is crumbly. Add the sour cream and mix with a fork until the dough clings together and begins to leave the sides of the bowl.
2. Gather the dough in a ball and knead several times. Wrap it in wax paper and chill for several hours or overnight.
3. Preheat the oven to 375°F.
4. To make filling, measure the pineapple into one cup. Reserve ½ cup of the pineapple juice and combine with the cornstarch, sugar, nutmeg, cloves, and cinnamon in a small saucepan. Mix well and stir in the blackberries.
5. Bring to a boil, stirring constantly. Let boil, uncovered, for 1 minute. Remove from the heat and stir in crushed pineapple; cool.
6. Divide the dough in half. Keeping half in the refrigerator until ready to use, roll out the other half to a 15 x 10-inch rectangle. Trim the edges even with scissors or a sharp knife. Cut into six 5-inch squares.
7. Place about 2 tablespoons of Blackberry-Pineapple Filling in each square, moisten the edges with water, and fold over to make a

triangle. Crimp the edges with a fork to seal and place on an ungreased cookie sheet. Repeat with the remaining dough.

8. Make 1 or 2 gashes in each turnover to let steam escape, then sprinkle with granulated sugar. Bake in the preheated oven for 25 minutes.
9. Serve warm.

Makes 1 dozen.

BLACKBERRY WINE TARTS

¼ cup honey
½ cup dry red wine
3 cups blackberries
Cornstarch
1 teaspoon vanilla extract
1 tablespoon kirsch
½ cup sliced, toasted almonds
8 prebaked Tart Shells (page 20)
½ cup cream, whipped, or 1 cup whipped topping

1. Combine the honey and wine in a saucepan. Add the berries and simmer, uncovered, for 5 minutes. Remove the fruit from the syrup and set aside.
2. Pour the syrup out of the saucepan and measure; for every cup of syrup dissolve 1 tablespoon of cornstarch. Return the syrup and cornstarch mixture to the saucepan and cook until thick and clear. Let the syrup cool.
3. Add the fruit, vanilla, kirsch, and nuts to the cooled liquid, then pour into the tart shells and chill.
4. Top with whipped cream just before serving.

Serves 8.

BLACKBERRY COBBLER

A cobbler is an old-fashioned dish that does very nicely for modern people in a hurry. Much easier to make than pie, it provides the same juicy satisfaction with a "dough" that needs no rolling, patting, or shaping. Try this on a busy day when you have a hankering for a home-baked dessert.

Blueberries or raspberries may be substituted.

Berry Mixture

1 pint blackberries
⅓ cup granulated sugar
1 teaspoon ground cinnamon
1 teaspoon grated lemon rind
¾ cup water

Batter

1 cup sifted all-purpose flour
1½ teaspoons baking powder
⅛ teaspoon salt
¼ cup (½ stick) butter or margarine
½ cup granulated sugar
1 egg, lightly beaten
⅓ cup milk
1½ teaspoons vanilla extract

1. Preheat the oven to 375°F. Grease a 1½-quart baking dish.
2. Combine the berries, ⅓ cup sugar, cinnamon, lemon rind, and water. Bring to a boil, stirring continually until the sugar dissolves. Reduce the heat and let simmer, uncovered, for 5 minutes.
3. Sift together the flour, baking powder, and salt. Set aside.
4. Cream the butter or margarine until soft, gradually adding ½ cup sugar and beating after each addition until the mixture is light and fluffy.

5. Add the dry ingredients and creamed butter alternately with the combined egg, milk, and vanilla to the berry mixture, beating well after each addition. The batter will be thin.
6. Pour the hot berry mixture into the greased baking dish and spoon on the cobbler batter. Bake in the preheated oven for 30 minutes, or until the cobbler is nicely browned.
7. Serve warm, with vanilla ice cream or whipped cream.

Serves 6.

ORANGE-BLACKBERRY JAM

1 quart blackberries
3½ cups granulated sugar
Juice of ½ orange
1 tablespoon grated orange peel
1 tablespoon ground cinnamon
⅛ teaspoon ground nutmeg
One 6-ounce bottle liquid pectin

1. In a kettle cook the berries, sugar, orange juice, and grated orange peel until heated through.
2. Sieve half of the berries to remove their seeds and return the puree mixture to the kettle. Add the cinnamon and nutmeg and bring to a full boil. Boil for 1 minute, stirring constantly. Stir in the pectin.
3. Remove from the heat and skim off the foam. Pour the hot jam into hot, sterilized half-pint jars and seal according to the directions on pages 11 and 12.

Makes about 5 half-pints.

PUNGENT BLACKBERRY CHUTNEY

Blackberries will find their way to the main course of a dinner in this spicy relish. Serve as an accompaniment to fish or fowl.

1 pound tart apples
2 pounds blackberries
2 cups malt vinegar
1 cup raisins
⅛ teaspoon cayenne pepper
2 tablespoons salt
1 teaspoon ground ginger
1 cup loosely packed brown sugar
2 teaspoons mustard seed

1. Remove the cores from the apples but do not peel them. Grind them by hand or in a blender and add them to the berries, which have been crushed slightly. Place mixture in a large saucepan.
2. Add the vinegar and let simmer for 30 minutes.
3. Mash the fruit through a sieve and add the remaining ingredients, all except the brown sugar and mustard seed.
4. Simmer for 5 minutes and add the brown sugar, then simmer again for about 25 minutes.
5. Add the mustard seed. Pour the mixture into sterilized jars, seal, and process in a boiling water bath (page 12). Or you may store covered in the refrigerator if you plan to use within a 2-week period.

Makes about 2½ pints.

BLACKBERRY-APRICOT PINNACLE

2 cups apricot nectar
⅔ cup fresh lemon juice
½ cup confectioners' sugar
2½ cups cold water
Cracked ice
1 cup blackberries

1. Combine the nectar, lemon juice, sugar, and water in a bowl or pitcher and stir well.
2. Add cracked ice to 4 tall glasses.
3. Pour the liquid over the ice and carefully stir ¼ cup of blackberries into each drink.
4. Serve with long-stemmed spoons.

Serves 4.

PURPLE PASSION PUNCH

2 cups pineapple juice
2 cups blackberry juice (page 28)
2 cups strong, chilled tea
3 quarts lemon-lime soda
Ice cubes
Pineapple slices
1 pint blackberries

1. Combine the juices and tea; chill.
2. When ready to serve, add the soda and ice cubes and float pineapple slices and blackberries on top of the punch mixture.

Fills about 20 punch cups.

BLACKBERRY JUICE

2 quarts blackberries
1 tablespoon water

1. Place the berries in a kettle with the water. Cook over medium heat, stirring frequently, until the berries are soft (about 10 minutes).
2. Strain through a jelly bag or several layers of cheesecloth.

Makes about 2 cups.

HOT RUSSIAN PUNCH

1 quart blackberry juice (double the recipe above)
1 cup orange juice
1 cup brewed orange pekoe tea
2 whole cloves
1 tablespoon whole allspice
1 tablespoon lemon juice
2 inches stick cinnamon
Vodka (about 2 cups; the amount will vary according to your taste)
10 strips lemon peel, approximately

1. Mix the juices and tea and add the cloves, allspice, lemon juice, and cinnamon. Simmer briefly, for about 3 minutes.
2. Add the vodka. Serve hot, with lemon peel floating in each cup.

Fills about 24 punch cups.

BERRY GOOD BREAKFAST

Sip summertime through a straw by drinking your berries in any number of nutritious ways—try this one.

Blueberries, currants, elderberries, gooseberries, mulberries, raspberries, or strawberries may be substituted for blackberries.

2 cups plain yogurt
1 pint blackberries
1 tablespoon honey, or to taste

1. Blend all the ingredients until smooth. Sieve the liquid to remove seeds, if you wish.
2. Pour into tall glasses to serve.

Serves 2.

BLACKBERRY LEAF TEA

The usefulness of blackberries is extended even to their leaves, which make a tasty tea.

Blueberry, raspberry, and strawberry leaves may be substituted.

To Dry Leaves: Wash gently and towel dry. Place in a single layer on fine mesh in a dark, warm, dust-free area. You can also make bags out of mesh and hang your leaves to dry from these. Store the leaves, when they have dried, in airtight glass jars, crumbling them, if necessary, to fit into the containers.

To Make Tea: Steep 1 to 2 teaspoons of dried berry leaves to each cup of hot water for 3 to 10 minutes.

Note: Sweeten your tea as Europeans do, with 1 teaspoon of jam or jelly for each cup of tea. Use berry jam in berry leaf tea to make the very most of your berries!

BLACKBERRY CORDIAL

I've saved this for the last because you might well serve it as the last course of a memorable dinner. The word "cordial" means "of the heart," and blackberry cordial is an old-fashioned liqueur that has warmed many a heart.

To bottle the liqueur, use interestingly shaped small bottles. Salad dressing containers, well washed and dried, can serve this purpose.

1 pint blackberries
3 cups brandy
3 inches stick cinnamon
6 whole cloves
1½ cups water
½ cup granulated sugar

1. Crush the berries and put them, with their juice, into a jar with 2 cups of the brandy and the spices. Shake well, then seal tightly and let steep for 1 week.
2. Pour through a wire strainer several times and then strain through a jelly bag (see page 11).
3. Bring the water and sugar to a rolling boil; cook until the sugar dissolves. Add to the berry juice, along with the rest of the brandy.
4. Bottle and seal.

Makes about 2 pints.

Note: There's no need to age this drink; it's ready to be enjoyed immediately after bottling.

BLUE-BERRIES

You ought to have seen what I saw on my way
To the village, through Patterson's pasture today:
Blueberries as big as the end of your thumb,
Real sky-blue, and heavy, and ready to drum
In the cavernous pail of the first one to come!
And all ripe together, not some of them green
and some of the ripe! You ought to have seen!

—From "Blueberries"
by ROBERT FROST

Who is there who doesn't love the blueberry? It is a true cook's delight, for it can be eaten fresh; combines deliciously with a number of other fruits; cheerfully adapts itself to all kinds of cakes, muffins, and breads; and adds its distinctive blue touch to menus that are otherwise notably nonblue.

Highest of all berries in vitamin A content, blueberries can be stored without spoiling for as long as 2 weeks in the refrigerator if they are dry and well covered. They freeze just as easily; see the general directions on pages 8 and 9.

Blueberries are true American natives, and were here to greet and help sustain the Pilgrims after they landed in Massachusetts. They were heavily used by the Indians, who often dried them, beat them into a powder, and added meal for a dish they called *sauta thig*. The Indians used them also with wild rice and venison and in a sweet bread called *wo-ja-pi* (see the recipe on page 45).

This modest and charming little berry has become such a staple that it is grown commercially in many parts of the United States and in Canada as well. Small, tangy wild blueberries, which many people feel are the tastiest of all, are found most often in Maine.

You can find blueberries, canned and frozen, all year round in your supermarket:

One 16-ounce package of frozen, unsweetened blueberries = 1½ pints (3 cups) fresh blueberries

One 15-ounce can blueberries in syrup = 1 cup berries, 1 cup syrup

One 21-ounce can blueberry pie filling = 2 cups of berries in thick sauce

When using blueberries in batters, be sure they are especially well drained. Tossing them in a little flour beforehand will help keep them from staining the batter.

The huckleberry can be used like the blueberry, although its impact on literature, through Mark Twain's classic *Huckleberry Finn*, has been greater than its impact on cuisine. Huckleberries are filled inside with large, crunchy seeds, which is why they are sometimes referred to as "crackerberries."

The European counterpart of the blueberry is the bilberry, which can be prepared like its American cousin. But love of blueberries has now spread abroad, and they are a feature of many European recipes, as samples in this collection will show.

BLUEBERRY-WINE SOUP

Serve this and other berry soups in bowls that have been well chilled. Nestle them in slightly larger bowls that have been lined with crushed ice for a refreshing way to stimulate appetites on even the stickiest of summer days.

1½ quarts blueberries
3½ tablespoons cornstarch
½ cup cold water
½ cup granulated sugar or to taste
Dash each of ground cinnamon and freshly grated nutmeg
½ cup port wine
Plain yogurt and grated orange peel for garnish

1. Place the berries in a saucepan and add enough water to just cover them. Bring to a boil and simmer, uncovered, until the berries become quite soft. Put the mixture through a sieve and return to the saucepan.
2. Dissolve the cornstarch in ½ cup cold water and stir into the soup. Add the sugar, cinnamon, and nutmeg. Cook, stirring all the while, until the mixture comes to a full boil; continue to boil without stirring for 5 minutes.
3. Remove from the heat and stir in the wine. Refrigerate until chilled.
4. Serve topped with dollops of yogurt and sprinkled with grated orange peel.

Serves 6 to 8.

ZUPA JAGODOWA

This is served in Poland after the meat course at dinner and is often accompanied by cold noodles. Nut Dumplings (page 15) are another tasty accompaniment.

4 cups water
1 quart blueberries
1 slice white bread
1 teaspoon ground cinnamon
¼ teaspoon ground cloves
1 egg, well beaten
½ cup granulated sugar
⅔ cup plain yogurt

1. Bring the water to a boil. Add the berries, bread, cinnamon, cloves, and egg. Simmer, uncovered, for 15 minutes.
2. Put through a sieve. Add the sugar and chill thoroughly before serving. Garnish with plain yogurt.

Serves 6 to 8.

OATMEAL-BLUEBERRY PANCAKES

1½ cups whole-wheat flour
1 cup rolled oats
2 tablespoons granulated sugar
2 teaspoons baking powder
¼ teaspoon salt
2 cups milk
2 eggs
1 cup blueberries, well drained after washing and dredged in a little flour

1. Combine the flour, oats, sugar, baking powder, and salt in a large bowl. In another bowl beat the milk and eggs until well mixed.
2. Combine the wet and dry ingredients. Gently fold in the berries.
3. Using ¼ cup batter for each pancake, bake on a hot, greased griddle until golden brown on both sides.
4. Serve immediately topped with butter and maple syrup.

Makes 15 pancakes.

NORWEGIAN BLUEBERRY OMELET

Omelet

8 eggs, separated
½ cup cream or milk
½ teaspoon salt
4 tablespoons (½ stick) butter or margarine
½ cup granulated sugar
1 tablespoon grated lemon peel

Blueberry Sauce

1 pint blueberries
½ cup granulated sugar
1 tablespoon lemon juice
1 tablespoon cornstarch
½ cup cold water

1. Beat the egg whites until stiff but not dry.
2. In another bowl beat the yolks until thick and lemon colored. Beat in the cream and salt; fold in the beaten egg whites.
3. Melt the butter or margarine in a heavy frying pan about 10 inches in diameter. Add the eggs to the pan and cook slowly over low heat until they are golden brown on the bottom—this should take about 10 minutes.
4. Meanwhile, preheat the oven to 350°F.
5. Place the omelet in the preheated oven and bake for about 10 minutes, or until done on the inside.
6. While the omelet is baking, make the sauce. Combine the berries, sugar, and lemon juice in a saucepan. Bring to a boil and let boil, uncovered, for 2 minutes. Dissolve the cornstarch in the cold water and add to the berries. Let boil for another minute.
7. Loosen the omelet from the pan and turn out into a shallow baking pan. Make a slash in the middle of the omelet with a knife and sprinkle the top with the sugar mixed with the lemon peel.
8. Place under the broiler for a few moments, until the sugar melts and the omelet browns slightly. Pour some of the blueberry sauce over the omelet and serve at once. Pass the remaining sauce separately.

Serves 4.

BLUEBERRY BLINTZES

Here is a traditional Jewish dish that may be served at breakfast, lunch, or dinner or as the star of an after-theater treat.

Blackberries, raspberries, or strawberries may be substituted.

Batter

1 cup sifted all-purpose flour
½ teaspoon salt
4 eggs
1 cup milk
Butter or margarine for frying

Filling

1 pint blueberries
2 tablespoons granulated sugar, or to taste
2 tablespoons all-purpose flour

1. Sift together the flour and salt. In a separate bowl beat the eggs and milk together.
2. Gradually add the flour to the egg mixture, stirring constantly. Let the mixture stand for at least 1 hour.
3. Heat a 6-inch skillet over moderately high heat and then lightly coat with butter or margarine. Fill a measuring cup with batter and pour about ½ cupful into the pan. As soon as the batter sticks to the pan, pour the excess back into the cup. (This ensures the proper thinness to your blintzes; traditionally, they must be thin enough so the cook can easily read a Yiddish newspaper through them!)
4. Fry until the blintz begins to blister and the edges begin to curl away from the pan. Turn out, fried side up, by inverting the pan over a wooden board. When all the blintzes are fried, separate them by stacking them between pieces of wax paper.
5. Mix all the filling ingredients together, then place 1 tablespoon filling in the center of each blintz (on the browned side).
6. Raise the bottom flap of the blintz to cover the filling, then fold over both sides so they almost meet at the center. Overlap the top flap to form a neat, enclosed envelope.
7. Fry the blintzes in a generous amount of butter or margarine until nicely browned on both sides.
8. Serve hot, with cold sour cream or hot Blueberry Sauce used in the Norwegian Blueberry Omelet (page 35).

Makes about 1 dozen.

HANUKKAH LATKES WITH BLUEBERRIES

Hanukkah is often celebrated with potato pancakes, but here are latkes made of flour and matzoh meal, in which juicy berries are stacked. A fine way to use frozen blueberries in midwinter.

2 cups sifted all-purpose flour
1 tablespoon baking powder
1 tablespoon granulated sugar
½ teaspoon salt
2 tablespoons matzoh meal
1½ cups milk
3 eggs, well beaten
¼ cup (½ stick) melted butter or margarine
4 cups blueberries in syrup

1. Sift together the flour, baking powder, sugar, and salt. Stir in the matzoh meal.
2. Combine the milk and eggs in a separate bowl and then mix them into the dry ingredients. Stir in the melted butter or margarine and beat until smooth.
3. Using ⅛ cup of batter for each pancake, cook on a hot, greased griddle until golden brown on both sides. Keep warm.
4. Heat the blueberries gently. Spread the latkes with additional butter. Put together in stacks of three, with blueberries in between and on top.
5. Serve at once.

Makes about 18 latkes.

PILGRIM'S CASSEROLE

It was food like this, fresh from the earth of the New World, that gave the Pilgrims cause for celebration. Delicious with fowl, pork, or ham.

6 medium sweet potatoes
1 pint blueberries
1 teaspoon orange juice
½ cup packed light brown sugar
1 tablespoon grated lemon rind
1 cup chopped walnuts
Dash each of ground cinnamon and salt
¼ cup (½ stick) cold butter or margarine, cut up
¼ cup lemon juice

1. Preheat the oven to 350°F. Grease a 1½-quart ovenproof casserole.
2. Cook the potatoes in boiling water to cover for about 15 minutes; then peel and cut into small pieces. Place half of the pieces in the prepared baking dish.
3. Scatter 1 cup of the berries, mixed with the orange juice, over the potatoes in the baking dish. Over this spread half of the brown sugar, the lemon rind, and ½ cup of the nuts. Sprinkle with dashes of cinnamon and salt.
4. Repeat the layers, then top the casserole with pats of butter or margarine. Pour the lemon juice over all and bake in the preheated oven for 1 hour.

Serves 4 to 6.

FRUITED HAM AND BLUEBERRY SALAD

A delightful combination of tastes from the North American Blueberry Council.

Salad greens, cut into bite-sized pieces
3 cups diced, cooked smoked or boiled ham
2 cups fresh orange sections
1 cup sliced celery
1 pint blueberries
Ruby French Dressing (below)

1. Line a salad bowl with the greens. Arrange the ham, oranges, celery, and blueberries in an attractive pattern over the greens and chill.
2. Just before serving, toss with the French dressing.

Serves 6.

RUBY FRENCH DRESSING

⅔ cup salad oil
⅓ cup red wine vinegar
½ teaspoon salt
2 teaspoons paprika
1 teaspoon dry mustard

Combine all the ingredients in a jar with a tight-fitting lid. Shake until well blended.

Makes 1 cup.

TART AND TANGY BLUEBERRY-LEMON MOLD

Topped with mayonnaise, this is a good accompaniment to chicken.

One 3-ounce package lemon gelatin
3 cups boiling water
1 cup sour cream
Two 3-ounce packages raspberry gelatin
One 15-ounce can of blueberries

1. Dissolve the lemon gelatin in 1 cup of the boiling water. Let cool, then stir in the sour cream. Refrigerate in a 6-cup mold until set.
2. Dissolve both packages of raspberry gelatin in the remaining 2 cups of boiling water; let cool. Drain the syrup from the blueberries, adding water if necessary to make 1 cup of liquid. Reserve the berries. Add the juice to the raspberry gelatin and stir. Pour the blueberry-raspberry mixture into the mold over the firm lemon gelatin.
3. When partially set, very carefully fold the reserved blueberries into the blueberry-raspberry gelatin, being careful not to disturb the lemon layer on the bottom. Unmold to serve.

Serve 6 to 8.

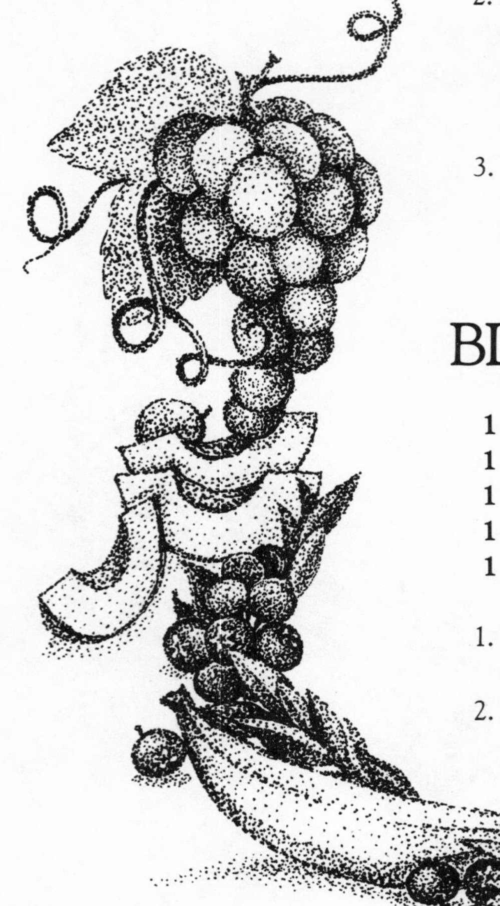

BLUEBERRY POTPOURRI

1 cup blueberries
1 small banana, sliced
1 cup sliced strawberries
1 peach, sliced
1 cup halved seedless grapes
2 cups watermelon cubes
2 tablespoons orange juice
Orange-Yogurt Dressing (page 17)

1. Mix all the fruits with the orange juice. Refrigerate until ready to serve.
2. Place the salad in small bowls and spoon the dressing over each serving.

Serves 6 to 8.

RED, WHITE, AND BLUEBERRY AMBROSIA

Here blueberries lend their color to a patriotic and festive dish that doubles both as a salad and as a dessert.

1 cup drained pineapple chunks
1 cup maraschino cherries
1 cup blueberries
2 cups diced marshmallows
1 cup sour cream
1 tablespoon confectioners' sugar

1. Combine all the ingredients, distributing them evenly.
2. Refrigerate for at least 1 hour.

Serves 6 *to* 8.

BLUEBERRY-CANTALOUPE SALAD

Serve this with iced tea and crunchy rolls with butter for a refreshing hot summer's day luncheon.

2 small cantaloupe melons
Leaf lettuce
1½ cups creamed cottage cheese
1 cup blueberries
Blueberry Dressing (page 42)

1. Halve the melons. Remove their seeds and scoop out the pulp with a melon baller.
2. Line each melon half with lettuce leaves. Place one-quarter of the melon balls in each melon shell.
3. Place about ⅓ cup cottage cheese in the center of each shell, and sprinkle ¼ cup of blueberries over.
4. Drizzle with the blueberry dressing and serve.

Serves 4.

BLUEBERRY DRESSING

⅓ cup blueberry jam
one 3-ounce package cream cheese, softened
1 tablespoon milk
½ teaspoon grated orange peel
2 teaspoons orange juice
¼ cup heavy cream, whipped, or ½ cup whipped topping

1. Blend the blueberry jam into the cream cheese. Add the milk, orange peel, and orange juice.
2. Blend the whipped cream into the cream cheese mixture and serve as a salad dressing.

Makes 1½ cups.

BESSIE'S BROWN SUGAR-BLUEBERRY MUFFINS

1½ cups sifted all-purpose flour
¼ teaspoon salt
1 tablespoon baking powder
1 egg, well beaten
¾ cup loosely packed light brown sugar
½ cup milk
1 tablespoon melted butter or margarine
1½ cups blueberries, well drained after washing and dredged in a little flour

1. Preheat the oven to 425°F. Grease a muffin tin or tins.
2. Sift together the flour, salt, and baking powder.
3. Combine the egg, brown sugar, milk, and butter or margarine, then mix into the dry ingredients. Stir with a fork until the mixture is moist but still lumpy. Fold in the blueberries.
4. Fill the greased muffin tins two-thirds full and bake in the preheated oven for 15 minutes, or until done.

Makes about 1 dozen.

WHOLE WHEAT-YOGURT-BLUEBERRY MUFFINS

1¾ cups whole-wheat flour
½ teaspoon salt
2 teaspoons baking powder
2 eggs, well beaten
½ cup granulated sugar
¾ cup plain yogurt
¼ cup (½ stick) butter or margarine, melted
1½ cups blueberries, well drained after washing and dredged in a little flour

1. Preheat the oven to 400°F. Grease a muffin tin or tins.
2. Sift together the flour, salt, and baking powder.
3. Combine the eggs, sugar, yogurt, and melted butter or margarine; mix into the dry ingredients. Stir with a fork until the mixture is moist but still lumpy. Fold in the berries.
4. Fill the greased muffin tins two-thirds full and bake in the preheated oven for about 25 minutes.

Makes about 1 dozen.

PINEAPPLE-BLUEBERRY BREAD

Sliced and buttered, this is a treat any time of the day! Cranberries, chopped and rolled in a little sugar, may be substituted.

½ cup (1 stick) butter or margarine
1⅓ cups granulated sugar
4 eggs, well beaten
1½ teaspoons lemon juice
3 cups all-purpose flour
2 teaspoons baking powder
1 teaspoon baking soda
¼ teaspoon salt
½ cup milk
1 cup crushed pineapple, well drained
1 pint blueberries, well drained after washing and dredged in a little flour
1 cup chopped nuts

1. Preheat the oven to 350°F. Grease and flour two or three loaf pans.
2. Cream the butter or margarine until very light; add the sugar. Beat well, then stir in the eggs and lemon juice. Add the combined flour, baking powder, soda, and salt alternately with the milk.
3. Stir in the pineapple, blueberries, and nuts, then place the batter in the greased and floured pans.
4. Bake in the preheated oven for 40 to 50 minutes. Let cool before cutting.

Makes 2 to 3 loaves.

WO-JA-PI

An American Indian sweet bread that comes recommended by the North American Blueberry Council.

Sauce

1 quart blueberries
1 cup honey
¼ cup unsifted all-purpose flour
1 cup cold water
2 tablespoons chopped fresh mint leaves

Fried Bread

2 cups sifted all-purpose flour
2 teaspoons baking powder
½ teaspoon salt
2 tablespoons granulated sugar
1 cup milk, more as needed
Deep fat or oil heated to 375°F

1. In a saucepan combine the berries, honey, and enough water to just cover the berries. Bring mixture to a boil and boil for 5 minutes.
2. In a bowl mix the flour with 1 cup of cold water until smooth. Stir the mixture into the hot berries. Add the mint and stir over low heat until the sauce thickens. Cool.
3. To make the bread, combine the flour, baking powder, salt, and sugar in a bowl. Stir in the milk until a soft dough is formed. It may be necessary to add a little more milk.
4. Knead the dough on a floured surface a few times until it is smooth. Roll out to a thickness of ½ inch and cut with a sharp knife into 3-inch squares.
5. Fry the squares in the preheated deep fat or oil until brown, about 3 to 4 minutes. Turn and brown on the other side. Drain on absorbent paper.
6. Serve warm, with the cooled blueberry sauce spooned on top.

Serves 8.

COUNTRY-STYLE CORNBREAD

Cranberries, chopped and rolled in a little sugar, may be substituted.

½ cup (1 stick) butter or margarine
1 cup granulated sugar
2 eggs
1 cup yellow corn meal
1½ cups all-purpose flour
¼ teaspoon salt
1½ teaspoons baking powder
1½ cups milk
1 cup blueberries, well drained after washing and dredged in a little flour

1. Preheat the oven to 375°F. Grease an 8-inch square baking pan.
2. Cream the butter or margarine with the sugar. Add the eggs and corn meal and beat well. Sift the flour, salt, and baking powder onto a sheet of waxed paper.
3. Add one-third of the flour mixture to the corn meal mixture, then ½ cup of milk. Beat. Repeat twice until you have used all of the milk.
4. Stir in the blueberries, then pour the batter into the prepared pan and bake in the preheated oven for 40 minutes, or until the bread tests done. Serve warm.

Serves 6.

BERRIED TREASURE

1 pint blueberries
1 pint strawberries
1½ tablespoons cherry liqueur
1 tablespoon granulated sugar
½ cup heavy cream, whipped

1. Place the blueberries and strawberries in a bowl and pour in the cherry liqueur. Cover and refrigerate for at least 1 hour to marinate.
2. When ready to serve, divide the berries among 4 dessert dishes or long-stemmed glasses. Fold the sugar into the whipped cream and garnish each portion with a dollop.

Serves 4.

RED, WHITE, AND BLUEBERRY BARS

Blueberries, strawberries, and yogurt combine healthfully in this freezer dessert.

One 14-ounce can sweetened condensed milk
⅓ cup lime juice
2 teaspoons grated lime peel
2 cups plain yogurt
2 cups miniature marshmallows
½ cup chopped nuts
1 pint strawberries, sliced
1 cup blueberries, well drained after washing

1. In a large bowl combine the sweetened condensed milk, lime juice, and grated peel. Mix well and stir in the yogurt, marshmallows, and nuts.
2. Add half the mixture to a 13 x 9-inch baking pan. Arrange half of the strawberries and blueberries over this, then cover with the remaining milk mixture and then the rest of the fruit.
3. Cover well with foil and place in the freezer until firm.
4. Remove from the freezer 10 minutes before cutting.

Makes 16.

BLUEBERRIES IN LIQUEUR

1 pint blueberries
2 tablespoons fruit-flavored liqueur
½ cup heavy cream, whipped
½ teaspoon almond extract

1. Place the berries in a bowl and sprinkle the liqueur over them. Chill for at least 1 hour to marinate.
2. Blend the berries with the whipped cream and almond extract just before serving.

Serves 4.

BLUEBERRY-LIME SOUFFLE

2 envelopes unflavored gelatin
½ cup granulated sugar
4 eggs, separated
2¼ cups water
1 tablespoon grated lime rind
½ cup lime juice
2 cups blueberries, well drained after washing
½ cup heavy cream, whipped
Lime slices for garnish

1. Combine the gelatin and half of the sugar in a medium saucepan. Beat the egg yolks, mix with the water, and add to the gelatin. Place over low heat and stir until the gelatin is dissolved.
2. Remove from the heat, add the lime rind and juice, and mix well. Chill until the mixture is partially thickened.
3. Beat the egg whites until they reach the soft-peak stage. Gradually add the remaining sugar and whip until stiff but not dry.
4. Add the gelatin mixture and mix well. Fold in the blueberries and whipped cream, making sure they are well blended.
5. Pour the mixture into a 1½-quart soufflé dish with a 2-inch collar. Chill until firm.
6. Remove the collar when ready to serve and garnish with slices of fresh lime.

Serves 6.

BLUEBERRY BETTY

1 cup all-purpose flour
1 cup packed light brown sugar
½ cup quick-cooking oats
¼ teaspoon ground mace
½ teaspoon ground cinnamon
½ cup (1 stick) butter or margarine
1 quart blueberries

1. Preheat the oven to 400°F. Grease a 9-inch square baking pan.
2. Mix together the flour, sugar, oats, mace, and cinnamon. Cut in the butter or margarine with a pastry blender or two knives until the mixture resembles coarse crumbs.
3. Place the berries in the prepared pan and sprinkle the oat mixture over. Bake in the preheated oven for 25 to 30 minutes, or until top is nicely browned.
4. Let cool slightly, then serve with ice cream or whipped cream.

Serves 6.

PETITE CHARLOTTES

"Come for dinner tonight!" exclaimed a friend of mine one Tuesday morning on the spur of the moment. Although she then worked all day, the meal was fine—a savory pot roast that had cooked all day in a crock-pot and this lovely little dessert. Although it could be fancied up, I include it here in its simplest form as a suggestion for dining that is both easy and memorable.

One 3¼-ounce package vanilla pudding mix
2 cups milk
8 lady fingers, split in half
1 cup blueberries, well drained after washing

1. Prepare the pudding as directed on the package, using the 2 cups of milk. Let cool until lukewarm.
2. Place 4 lady finger halves each in a star-shaped pattern in 4 shallow fruit dishes. Over this pour the cooled pudding, then sprinkle all over with the berries. Cover and refrigerate until ready to serve.

Serves 4.

BOSTON GINGERBREAD

This is an old-fashioned New England treat, delicious served with applesauce and whipped cream.

Cranberries, chopped and rolled in a little sugar, may be substituted.

¼ cup (½ stick) butter or margarine
½ cup granulated sugar
2 eggs, well beaten
1¾ cups all-purpose flour
1 teaspoon baking soda
⅛ teaspoon salt
1 teaspoon ground ginger
2 teaspoons ground cinnamon
½ cup sour cream
½ cup molasses
1½ cups blueberries, well drained after washing and dredged in a little flour

1. Preheat the oven to 350°F. Grease and lightly flour an 8-inch square baking pan.
2. Cream the butter or margarine. Add the sugar gradually and then the eggs. Beat well.
3. Sift together the dry ingredients and add alternately with the combined sour cream and molasses to the creamed mixture.
4. Fold in the berries, then pour the batter into the prepared 8-inch baking pan and bake in the preheated oven for 45 minutes.
5. Serve as is, or with applesauce and/or whipped cream.

Serves 6.

Variations:

1. Make gingerbread muffins by pouring the batter into greased and floured muffin tins. Bake at 350°F for 20 minutes, or until done.
2. Don't forget convenient gingerbread mixes if you're in a hurry! Just prepare according to package directions and fold in the blueberries before baking.

LEMON-BLUEBERRY CAKE

One 15-ounce can blueberries in syrup
One 18-ounce package lemon cake mix
1 cup sour cream
4 eggs
½ cup granulated sugar
1 tablespoon cornstarch
Confectioners' sugar

1. Preheat the oven to 350°F. Grease well and lightly flour a 10-inch tube pan.
2. Drain the blueberries, reserving 1 cup of the blueberry syrup. Rinse the berries and drain very well by placing them on absorbent paper.
3. In a large bowl combine the dry cake mix, sour cream, and eggs. Blend for 1 minute at low speed and then beat for 2 minutes at medium speed, scraping the sides of the bowl occasionally.
4. Fold in the blueberries, then pour the batter into the prepared tube pan and bake in the preheated oven for 35 to 40 minutes, or until the top springs back when touched lightly.
5. Cool the cake in the pan for 15 minutes, then remove from the pan and let cool completely.
6. While the cake is cooling, combine the sugar and cornstarch in a small saucepan over medium heat and gradually stir in the reserved syrup. Bring to a boil, stirring constantly until thickened.
7. Sprinkle the cooled cake with confectioners' sugar and serve, passing the sauce separately.

Serves 10 to 12.

EIGHT-LAYER BLUEBERRY CAKE

Something special from the North American Blueberry Council.

4 eggs
1 cup granulated sugar
½ cup water
1 teaspoon vanilla extract
1 cup sifted all-purpose flour
2 teaspoons baking powder
1 pint blueberries, well drained after washing and dredged in a little flour
1 cup heavy cream, whipped
⅓ cup confectioners' sugar
2 tablespoons orange liqueur

1. Preheat the oven to 375°F.
2. Beat the eggs until thick and lemon colored. Gradually beat in the sugar and whip until very thick.
3. Stir in the water and vanilla, then fold in the combined flour and baking powder.
4. Line two 8-inch layer-cake pans with foil. Grease the foil and spoon ¾ cup of the batter onto each foil-lined pan. Sprinkle ¼ cup of the blueberries over the batter in each pan.
5. Bake in the preheated oven for 12 minutes, or until the edges are lightly browned. Loosen the edges with a knife and turn out on racks. Carefully strip off the foil and let the cakes cool while you prepare the remaining layers.
6. Repeat the procedure until you have eight layers.
7. Beat the cream with the confectioners' sugar until stiff. Fold in the liqueur. Spread the cream between the cooled cake layers, leaving the top uncovered.
8. Ring the top of the cake with the remaining blueberries as decorations. Cut with a serrated-edged knife to serve.

Serves 6 to 8.

BLUEBERRY BUCKLE

Another fine old New England treatment of blueberries. Its crumb topping makes it especially good with coffee or tea.

Cake

2 eggs
½ cup (1 stick) butter or margarine, softened
¾ cup granulated sugar
2 cups all-purpose flour
2 teaspoons baking powder
½ teaspoon salt
½ cup milk
2 cups blueberries, well drained after washing and dredged in a little flour

Topping

½ cup granulated sugar
⅓ cup all-purpose flour
½ teaspoon ground cinnamon
¼ cup (½ stick) butter or margarine, softened

1. Preheat the oven to 350°F. Grease a 9-inch square baking pan.
2. Cream together the eggs, butter or margarine, and sugar. Sift together the flour, baking powder, and salt; then resift into the egg mixture alternately with the milk.
3. Fold in the blueberries and pour the batter into the prepared baking pan.
4. Combine all the topping ingredients and cut together with a pastry blender or two knives until crumbly. Spread over the batter and bake for 45 minutes, or until the cake tests done.

Makes 9 squares.

POLISH BLUEBERRY SQUARES

I've never heard a joke about Polish cooking, which is, I suppose, because everyone takes its goodness quite seriously. Here is a juicy and delightful way to use up a great many berries.

1 cup (2 sticks) butter or margarine
1¼ cups granulated sugar
4 eggs
2 cups all-purpose flour
1 teaspoon almond extract
2 teaspoons baking powder
1 teaspoon ground cinnamon
¼ teaspoon freshly grated nutmeg
1½ pints blueberries, drained well after washing and dredged in a little flour
¼ cup confectioners' sugar

1. Preheat the oven to 400°F. Grease a 9 x 12-inch baking pan, then sprinkle the bottom and sides with fine, dry bread crumbs.
2. Beat the butter or margarine with the sugar very well. Add the eggs alternately with the flour, then beat for 5 minutes more.
3. Fold in the almond extract, baking powder, cinnamon, and nutmeg, then spoon the batter into the prepared baking pan.
4. Sprinkle the blueberries on top. They will sink slightly into the batter during baking and thus become an integral part of the cake. Bake in the preheated oven for 45 minutes, or until the cake tests done.
5. Cool the cake. Just before serving, sprinkle the confectioners' sugar through a sieve over the top.

Makes 16.

PIE CRUST FOR BERRY DESSERTS

The sugar and orange juice make this an especially tasty crust for berry pies.

1 cup all-purpose flour
1 heaping teaspoon granulated sugar
6⅓ tablespoons butter or margarine
2 tablespoons *cold* orange juice
Ground cinnamon

1. Combine the flour and sugar, then add the butter or margarine to the flour mixture in small pieces. Blend the mixture with a pastry blender or two knives until it resembles coarse meal.
2. Sprinkle the cold orange juice evenly over the flour mixture and toss with a fork. The whole thing will begin to stick together, and you can help it on its way by using your hands, working quickly.
3. When the dough has been patted together into a cohesive ball, place it on floured wax paper or on a floured wooden cutting board. Roll out the pastry with a rolling pin that has been dusted with flour.
4. Fold the pastry in half or drape it over the rolling pin and place it gently in a pie plate. Unfold. Flute with your fingertips to make a decorative edge, then sprinkle the pastry with cinnamon. (At this point the crust is ready to be filled and baked according to a particular recipe for a single-crust pie; or you may prebake it, as described in the next step.)
5. To prebake, cover the edge with a 1½-inch strip of aluminum foil to prevent excessive browning. Prick the crust all over with a fork and fill it with dried beans to prevent air bubbles from forming. Bake it in a 475°F oven for 8 to 10 minutes, or according to the directions of your particular recipe.

Makes one 8- or 9-inch crust.

RED, WHITE, AND BLUEBERRY PIE

2 eggs
One 15-ounce can sweetened condensed milk
½ teaspoon grated lemon peel
½ cup fresh lemon juice
1 baked 9-inch pie shell (see Pie Crust for Berry Desserts, page 55) or crumb crust
2 tablespoons confectioners' sugar
1 cup heavy cream, whipped
1 pint strawberries, hulled
1 cup blueberries, well drained after washing
1 tablespoon silver dragees

1. Beat the eggs, condensed milk, and lemon peel together in a bowl. Gradually add the lemon juice. Beat until the mixture is thickened and pour into the pie shell. Refrigerate for 2 to 3 hours.
2. Stir the confectioners' sugar into the cream. Spread this mixture on top of the pie.
3. Place upstanding strawberries in circular pattern over the cream mixture. Sprinkle the blueberries and silver dragees in between, then refrigerate until ready to serve.

Serves 8.

JUICY BLUEBERRY PIE

1 quart blueberries
¾ cup granulated sugar, or to taste
⅓ cup all-purpose flour
1 teaspoon ground cinnamon
1½ teaspoons lemon juice
1½ teaspoons butter, cut up
Pastry for a Two-Crust Pie (page 20)

1. Preheat the oven to 425°F.
2. Combine the blueberries, sugar, flour, cinnamon, and lemon juice.

3. Roll out half the pastry and fit into a 9-inch pie pan. Pour the fruit mixture into the pastry shell and top with pats of butter. Cover with the remaining pastry, rolled out and cut into lattice strips or left in one piece for a top crust. Seal and flute the edges, then cut several slashes in the top crust, if using whole. Cover the edges of the crust with a 1½-inch strip of aluminum foil to prevent overbrowning.
4. Bake in the preheated oven for 35 to 40 minutes, or until the crust is golden brown and the juice begins to bubble through.

Serves 8.

BLUEBERRY GLACE PIE

Strawberries, blackberries, or raspberries may be substituted.

1 quart blueberries
¾ cup water
1 cup granulated sugar
3 tablespoons cornstarch
2 tablespoons orange juice
1 package (8 ounces) cream cheese, softened
1 baked 9-inch pie shell (page 55)

1. Simmer 1 cup of the berries in the water for 3 to 4 minutes. Combine the sugar and cornstarch and add to the cooking fruit, stirring all the while until the syrup is thick and ruby-clear. Stir in 1 tablespoon of the orange juice.
2. Mix the other tablespoon of orange juice with the softened cream cheese. Spread on the bottom of the pastry shell and cover with the remaining berries. Pour the cooked fruit mixture over all.
3. Chill the pie thoroughly before serving. This is especially tasty with ice cream or whipped cream.

Serves 8.

BLUEBERRY-PEACH COBBLER

If you've never before tasted the combination of blueberries and peaches (nectarines may be used in place of peaches), you're in for a rare treat. The piquant taste of blueberries goes deliciously with the mellow sweetness of peaches. The colors provide a pleasing contrast, too.

Fruit Mixture

1 cup blueberries
1½ cups sugared, sliced ripe peaches or nectarines
⅓ cup packed light brown sugar
2 teaspoons cornstarch
⅓ cup water
2 tablespoons butter or margarine
1½ teaspoons lemon juice

Batter

1 cup all-purpose flour
1 tablespoon granulated sugar
1½ teaspoons baking powder
½ teaspoon salt
3 tablespoons butter or margarine
½ cup milk

1. Preheat the oven to 400°F. Grease a 1-quart baking dish.
2. In a saucepan bring to a boil over moderate heat the blueberries, peaches or nectarines, brown sugar, and the cornstarch dissolved in the water. When the mixture begins to thicken, add the butter or margarine and the lemon juice.
3. Place in the prepared baking dish and set aside while you prepare the cobbler batter.
4. Sift the flour and stir it together with the sugar, baking powder, and salt. Cut in the shortening with a pastry blender until the mixture resembles coarse meal. Stir in the milk.
5. Drop the batter by spoonfuls onto the fruit mixture, then bake the cobbler 25 to 30 minutes in the preheated oven.
6. Serve warm, with cream, if desired.

Serves 4 to 6.

MINTED BLUEBERRY JAM

1 quart blueberries
3½ cups granulated sugar
Juice of 1 lemon
3 sprigs fresh mint
One 6-ounce bottle liquid pectin

1. In a large pan combine the blueberries, sugar, and lemon juice. Bring to a full boil and boil for 1 minute, stirring all the while. Remove from the heat, add the mint sprigs, and stir.
2. Stir in the pectin and skim off the foam. Remove the mint sprigs, then pour the hot jam into hot, sterilized half-pint jars.
3. Seal (see page 11) and store for up to 1 year in a cool, dry place.

Makes about 5 half-pints.

SPICY BLUEBERRY JELLY

2 quarts blueberries
1 cup water
6½ cups granulated sugar
1 tablespoon ground cinnamon
1 teaspoon ground cloves
3 ounces liquid pectin

1. Combine the blueberries and water in a preserving kettle and cook at a boil, uncovered, until the fruit is tender (about 10 minutes).
2. Strain through a cheesecloth that has been placed in a colander, or in a jelly bag (page 11), then return to the kettle.
3. Add the sugar, cinnamon, and cloves to the juice and bring to a boil. Stir in the pectin and continue to boil for 1 minute. Remove from the heat and skim off the foam.
4. Pour the jelly into hot, sterilized jelly glasses and seal (pages 10 and 11).

Makes about 10 medium glasses.

BLUEBERRY MINCEMEAT

Berries, apples, and zucchini form the base of this spicy relish. From the North American Blueberry Council.

½ cup water
1 tablespoon lemon juice
1 beef bouillon cube
3 green apples, unpeeled, cored and finely chopped
1 pint blueberries
2 medium zucchini, trimmed and finely chopped
2 tablespoons finely chopped orange peel
½ cup granulated sugar
½ teaspoon ground cinnamon
¼ teaspoon freshly grated nutmeg
2 envelopes unflavored gelatin
½ cup cold water

1. Combine the water, lemon juice, bouillon cube, apples, blueberries, zucchini, orange peel, sugar, and spices in a large saucepan. Cover and simmer for 30 minutes, stirring occasionally.
2. Stir the gelatin into the cold water. Stir this mixture into the hot mincemeat.
3. Spoon the mixture into jars, cover, and cool. Store in the refrigerator until ready to use.

Makes about 2 pints.

NEW HAMPSHIRE BLUEBERRY SHRUB

New Englanders have all sorts of wonderful ways with blueberries, and this one serves as a colorful base for drinks. Add ginger ale for a nonalcoholic beverage. Or combine with a shot of rum, gin, or bourbon for special potency.

5 quarts blueberries
1 quart cider vinegar
2 pounds granulated sugar, approximately

1. Crush the 5 quarts of berries and cover them for 24 hours with the cider vinegar. Store in a ceramic bowl or an enameled pot.
2. Crush the mixture again by lining a sieve or colander with cheesecloth and pressing the juice through this. To each quart of juice add 2 pounds of sugar.
3. Bring to a boil and let simmer, uncovered, for 15 minutes. Let cool.
4. Pour into sterilized bottles or jars, cap, and store in the refrigerator.

Makes about 1 quart.

LAVENDER COOLER

¼ cup granulated sugar
½ cup blueberries
1 ripe banana, peeled and cut into chunks
1 teaspoon lemon juice
1 pint vanilla ice cream, softened
1 quart milk, chilled

1. Place all the ingredients in a blender and blend until smooth.
2. Pour into tall, chilled glasses to serve.

Serves 4 to 6.

Far off in the fields, on the edge of a cranberry bog, stood the hut of the Cubbins family.

—From *The 500 Hats of Bartholomew Cubbins* by DR. SEUSS

That cranberries complement turkey is a truism that has long remained unchallenged in the American mind. Even during the heat of the Civil War, General Ulysses S. Grant insisted that cranberries be shipped to Union soldiers so they might enjoy them with their Thanksgiving meal. I don't quarrel with this, but I do think that cranberries have a right to a turkey-less identity of their own. When imaginatively used in breads, beverages, preserves, and desserts, these zesty berries can soar to heights of variety and deliciousness unforeseen by those who assign them rigidly to their predictable place beside the turkey.

They even have uses that go beyond the kitchen. You can pour them into a clear glass pitcher or vase along with several oranges for a striking and inexpensive centerpiece in autumn or winter. Unlike most other berries, the tough-skinned cranberry endures for long time periods at room temperature. Such a centerpiece brightened my dining room table for five weeks before the berries began to lose their shape and firmness.

Doctors prescribe cranberry juice as a remedy for cystitis, and American sailors once drank it as a preventative for scurvy, much as their British counterparts downed lime juice. The American Indians called cranberries *sassamanesh* and used them to make a rich, red dye.

Cranberries probably were named by settlers who noticed that their lovely red, pink, and white flowers resembled the outstretched neck of the crane in silhouette. A conflicting story tells how these berries attracted cranes, who swooped down in great numbers onto bogs in order to carry them off hungrily in their beaks. The origin of the word is still under debate, but the first explanation seems more likely, especially since cranes are not currently caught stealing the great abundance of cranberries that grow in Massachusetts, New Jersey, Washington, Oregon, and, most prolifically of all, in Wisconsin.

Cranberries begin to ripen in mid-September, thus making their appearance after the rest of the berries featured in these pages. They maintain another distinction by an extreme natural tartness that verges on bitterness. This situation is easily remedied, of course, by additions of sugar or honey. The cranberry is a cousin of the blueberry, and while the two are differently colored, you will notice that they share a hard outer skin that enables them to adapt well to baking and storage.

Indeed, because cranberries have the same happy facility as blueberries for blending into batters without discoloring them and without losing their own tangy flavor, they make good substitutes for blueberries in the breads featured in the last chapter. See especially Pineapple-Blueberry Bread (page 44), Boston Gingerbread (page 50), and Country Style Cornbread (page 46). When substituting cranberries for blueberries, just remember to cut them in half and roll them in a little sugar (brown or white can be used) to cut their natural bitterness.

You will find fresh cranberries in supermarkets only during the fall and winter, so it is a good idea to buy a few extra packages for the freezer.

1 pound fresh cranberries = 4 generous cups

One 16-ounce can whole cranberry sauce = 2 cups

One 32-ounce bottle of cranberry juice = 1 quart

CRANBERRY BORSCHT

A sassy variation on classic Russian beet borscht. Serve cold with warm boiled potatoes and crunchy rolls.

1 onion, minced
2 tablespoons butter
One 16-ounce can beets
3 cups water
3 chicken bouillon cubes
1 pound cranberries
1 tablespoon granulated sugar
¼ cup Madeira wine
1 teaspoon lemon juice
¼ teaspoon salt
Sour cream and chopped parsley for garnish (optional)

1. Sauté the onion in the butter until it is transparent. Meanwhile, drain and chop the beets, reserving their juice.
2. Puree the beets, beet juice, sauteed onion, and sauteing butter in a blender; remove to a bowl.
3. Combine the water, bouillon cubes, cranberries, and sugar and simmer for 10 minutes. Puree in the blender and add to the beet mixture.
4. Add the Madeira, lemon juice, and salt and mix well. Refrigerate until thoroughly chilled.
5. Serve with dollops of sour cream and a sprinkling of parsley, if desired.

Serves 4 to 6.

CRANBERRY-CARROT SOUP

6 cups commercial cranberry juice
1½ cups finely grated carrots
3 tablespoons potato starch
⅓ cup cold water

1. Heat the juice and carrots in a covered saucepan until hot but not boiling. Mix the starch with the water and then pour slowly into the juice. Bring to a boil, stirring continually.
2. Simmer until the soup thickens and the carrots become soft (about 5 minutes). Serve chilled.

Serves 4 to 6.

HARVEST-TIME PORK CHOPS

¼ cup cooking oil
8 pork chops, each ½ inch thick
Salt and freshly ground black pepper
½ cup light port wine
½ cup honey
1 teaspoon ground cinnamon
¼ teaspoon ground cloves
1½ cups cranberries, cut in half
1 green pepper, cut into slices

1. Heat the oil in a large skillet with a cover. Season the pork chops with salt and pepper and brown them well in the hot oil. Drain oil. Mix the port, honey, cinnamon, and cloves and pour over the pork chops. Cook, covered, for an hour, or until the meat is done.
2. About 5 minutes before you are ready to serve, add the cranberries and the green pepper. Simmer, uncovered, in the wine sauce until cooked through but still crisp.

Serves 4 to 6.

SWEET AND SOUR BERRIED MEATBALLS

Serve as an hors d'oeuvre or as a main dish over rice.

2 pounds lean ground beef
2 tablespoons soy sauce
2 tablespoons minced onion
2 eggs
2 cloves garlic, crushed, or 2 teaspoons garlic powder
1 cup crushed cornflakes
2 teaspoons salt
¼ teaspoon freshly ground black pepper
One 16-ounce can whole cranberry sauce
⅓ cup ketchup
2 tablespoons brown sugar
One 12-ounce bottle chili sauce
1 tablespoon lemon juice

1. Preheat the oven to 350°F.
2. Combine the ground beef, soy sauce, onion, eggs, garlic, cornflake crumbs, salt, and pepper in a large bowl. Mix well.
3. Shape the meat mixture into balls about the size of a large olive. Place in a large baking pan.
4. Combine the cranberry sauce, ketchup, brown sugar, chili sauce, and lemon juice in a small saucepan. Heat, stirring, until the cranberry sauce melts.
5. Pour the sauce over the meatballs and bake in the preheated oven for 45 minutes.

Makes about 60.

Variation: Substitute frankfurters for the meatballs and cut them into diagonal 1-inch chunks.

SABRINA'S CRANBERRY CHICKEN SQUARES

A refreshingly good way to use up leftover meats during the holidays.

Chicken Layer

1 envelope unflavored gelatin
¼ cup cold water
1 cup mayonnaise
½ cup lukewarm water
3 tablespoons lemon juice
½ teaspoon salt
2 cups diced chicken or turkey
½ cup diced celery
2 tablespoons chopped fresh parsley

Cranberry Layer

1 envelope unflavored gelatin
¼ cup cold water
One 16-ounce can whole cranberry sauce
One 9-ounce can crushed pineapple, drained
½ cup broken nuts
1 tablespoon lemon juice

Garnish

Crisp salad greens
Mayonnaise

1. Prepare the chicken layer first. Soften the gelatin in the cold water. Dissolve by setting bowl containing gelatin in slightly larger bowl or pan of water that has just boiled. Blend in the mayonnaise, ½ cup water, lemon juice, and salt. Add the chicken or turkey pieces, celery, and parsley. Pour into a 10 x 6 x 1½-inch baking dish and chill until firm.
2. To make the cranberry layer, soften the gelatin in cold water and dissolve over hot water as described in step 1. Stir in the remaining ingredients, then pour over the firm chicken layer and refrigerate until set.
3. Unmold on greens to serve and top with mayonnaise.

Serves 6 to 8.

COQ AU ROUGE

3 large whole chicken breasts, skinned, boned, and cut in half lengthwise
Salt and freshly ground black pepper
6 thin slices boiled ham
6 strips Swiss cheese
One 16-ounce can whole cranberry sauce
1 egg, beaten
¼ cup all-purpose flour
3 to 4 tablespoons butter
⅓ cup light port wine
2 tablespoons cornstarch
2 tablespoons cold water
1 cup sliced, toasted almonds

1. Preheat the oven to 350°F.
2. Pound the chicken breast halves into thin cutlets. Sprinkle with salt and pepper. Place the ham and cheese strips and 1 tablespoon of cranberry sauce on each cutlet and then roll up, jelly-roll fashion.
3. Coat first with egg and then roll in flour. Brown in butter over a low flame.
4. Place the chicken rolls in a baking dish. Combine the remaining cranberry sauce and the port wine and pour over, then cover and bake in the preheated oven for 1 hour.
5. Remove the chicken rolls to a platter and keep warm. Pour pan juices into a saucepan.
6. Combine the cornstarch and cold water and add to the pan juices, cooking quickly until thick. Spoon some of the sauce over the chicken and sprinkle with almonds. Pass the remaining sauce separately.

Serves 4 to 6.

BROWN RICE STUFFING WITH CRANBERRIES

1 cup raw brown rice
2 cups chicken broth
1¼ cups cranberries
3 tablespoons water
⅓ cup plus 2 tablespoons loose brown sugar
½ cup chopped celery
1 tablespoon butter
1 tablespoon chopped fresh parsley

1. Wash the rice and cook it, covered, in the chicken broth for 45 minutes on a low flame. Meanwhile, cook the cranberries, uncovered, in the water and brown sugar until they pop but are still whole. Brown the celery in the butter in a saucepan.
2. Mix together the berries and their syrup, the rice, celery, and parsley. Use as a stuffing or pass separately as a side dish.

Serves 4 *to* 6.

GINGER-BERRY MOLD

1 envelope unflavored gelatin
2 tablespoons cold water
One 16-ounce can jellied cranberry sauce
2 tablespoons lemon juice
1 cup ginger ale
¾ cup diced, unpeeled apple
¾ cup diced celery
½ cup chopped walnuts
Crisp salad greens and mayonnaise for garnish

1. In a cup, soften the gelatin in the cold water. Place the cup in a pan of water that has just boiled to dissolve the gelatin.
2. Crush the cranberry sauce with a fork and stir into the dissolved gelatin. Let cool slightly.
3. Add the lemon juice and ginger ale and mix well. Chill the mixture in the refrigerator until it begins to thicken.
4. Fold in the apple, celery, and walnuts, then turn into a 5-cup mold and chill until firm. Unmold; serve on greens topped with mayonnaise.

Serves 6.

CRANBERRY CRUNCH MOLD

Look no further for a large, tart, interestingly textured cranberry gelatin dish to serve with the main course at winter holiday feasts. Here it is!

1 orange, unpeeled, sliced and seeds removed
2 cups chopped cranberries
1 apple, unpeeled, cored and cut up
1 cup granulated sugar
1 cup boiling water
One 3-ounce package raspberry or lime gelatin
1 cup chopped celery
1 cup chopped walnuts
One 20-ounce can crushed pineapple, well drained
1 cup mayonnaise (optional)

1. Put the orange through a food grinder or grind it in a blender. Add to the chopped cranberries, the cut-up pieces of apple, and the sugar. Refrigerate for 1 hour.
2. Add the boiling water to the package of gelatin, along with the celery, nuts, and the well-drained pineapple. Add the cranberry mixture, pour into a 2-quart mold, and chill until firm.
3. Unmold onto a platter to serve. Garnish with mayonnaise, if desired.

Serves 12.

POLKA-DOT MUFFINS

3 cups all-purpose flour
1 tablespoon baking powder
1 teaspoon salt
¼ cup granulated sugar
1 teaspoon grated orange rind
½ cup shortening
1 egg, beaten
1 cup milk
1 cup cranberries, finely chopped

1. Preheat the oven to 425°F. Grease a muffin pan or pans.
2. Stir together the flour, baking powder, salt, sugar, and orange rind. Cut in the shortening with a pastry blender or a fork.

3. Mix together the egg and milk and then add to the flour-shortening mixture. Stir well.
4. Fold in the cranberries and fill each cup to the top. Bake in the preheated oven for 20 to 30 minutes.

Makes 1 dozen large muffins.

CRANBERRY-PUMPKIN BREAD

Blueberries, tossed in a little flour, can substitute for the cranberries in this recipe, except that they need not be chopped or rolled in sugar.

⅓ cup (5⅓ tablespoons) butter
1⅓ cups granulated sugar
2 eggs
½ teaspoon vanilla extract
1⅔ cups sifted all-purpose flour
¼ teaspoon baking powder
1 teaspoon baking soda
¾ teaspoon salt
1 teaspoon ground cinnamon
½ teaspoon freshly grated nutmeg
¼ teaspoon ground ginger
¼ teaspoon ground cloves
1 cup mashed, cooked pumpkin
1½ cups cranberries, chopped and rolled in ¼ cup sugar
1 cup chopped nuts

1. Preheat the oven to 350°F. Grease a 9 x 5 x 3-inch loaf pan.
2. Cream together the butter and sugar, then beat in the eggs and vanilla.
3. Sift together the dry ingredients. Add to the egg mixture and blend just until smooth.
4. Mix in the pumpkin, chopped and sugared berries, and nuts. Blend briefly. Pour into the greased loaf pan and bake in the preheated oven for 45 to 55 minutes, or until the bread tests done.

Makes 1 loaf.

CRANBERRY YULE LOGS

¾ cup finely chopped cranberries
½ cup water
½ cup granulated sugar
One 3-ounce package vanilla pudding mix
2 cups dairy eggnog
½ cup heavy cream
1 teaspoon rum extract
½ cup finely chopped toasted almonds

1. Cook the cranberries, uncovered, in the water and sugar for 5 minutes. Remove the berries and let them drain well on paper toweling.
2. Prepare the pudding mix according to package directions, using the eggnog in place of milk.
3. Whip the cream and fold it into the pudding mixture, along with the rum extract and the cranberries.
4. Turn the mixture into two 16-ounce fruit or vegetable cans. Cover and freeze for several hours or overnight.
5. To unmold, remove the bottoms of the cans and push the logs through. Roll the logs in toasted almonds. Before cutting, allow each one to stand at room temperature for about 10 minutes.

Serves 10 (each log makes 5 slices).

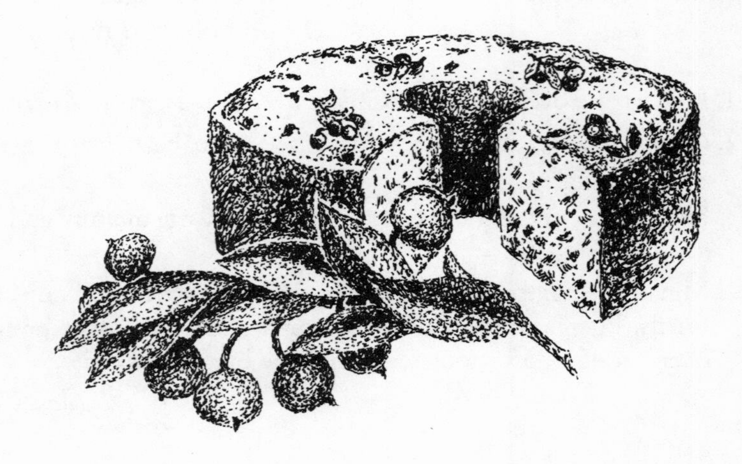

FESTIVAL FRUIT CAKE

1½ cups cranberries, cut in half
¼ cup loosely packed brown sugar
1 cup granulated sugar
2½ cups sifted all-purpose flour
¼ teaspoon salt
1 teaspoon baking soda
1 teaspoon baking powder
One 8-ounce package dates, pitted and quartered
2 tablespoons grated orange peel
1 cup chopped walnuts or pecans
2 eggs, beaten
¾ cup cooking oil
1 cup buttermilk or sour milk

Orange Juice Glaze

⅓ cup orange juice concentrate, thawed
⅓ cup granulated sugar

1. Preheat the oven to 350°F. Grease and flour a 10-inch tube pan.
2. Mix the cranberries with the brown sugar. Set aside.
3. Combine all the dry ingredients. Stir in the dates, sugared cranberries, orange peel, and nuts.
4. Combine the eggs, oil, and buttermilk and stir into the dry mixture. Pour the batter into the greased and floured tube pan and bake in the preheated oven for 1 hour or until the cake tests done.
5. Cool the cake in the pan for 10 minutes.
6. While the cake is cooling, mix the ingredients for the glaze in a small saucepan. Bring to a boil and boil gently for 5 minutes.
7. Invert the slightly cooled cake onto a serving plate. Brush with the orange juice glaze while still warm; the flavor of the transparent glaze will seep deliciously into the cake.

Makes 16 slices.

TWO-HEARTS CAKE

A Valentine's Day surprise.

One 9-ounce package (or half of a 16-ounce package) white cake mix
¾ cup boiling water
One 3-ounce package strawberry gelatin
One 16-ounce can whole cranberry sauce
Whipped cream

1. In an 8-inch heart-shaped cake pan, bake 1 layer of white cake mix as directed on the package. Unmold and let cool.
2. Add the boiling water to the gelatin. Stir to dissolve.
3. Stir the cranberry sauce in a separate bowl, then add it, well mixed, to the gelatin. Pour into an 8-inch heart-shaped cake pan and refrigerate until set.
4. Unmold the cranberry-strawberry layer onto the white cake layer. Trim the edges of the heart-shaped dessert with piping of whipped cream and serve.

Serves 8.

CRANBERRY-TOPPED CHEESECAKE

2 cups cranberries
1 cup granulated sugar
1 cup sweetened cranberry juice or cranberry juice cocktail
1 envelope unflavored gelatin
1 baked cheesecake (see Tilda's Strawberry Cheesecake, page 157)

1. Bring the cranberries, sugar, and ¾ cup of the juice to a boil. Reduce the heat and let simmer, uncovered, for 5 minutes.
2. Combine the gelatin with the remaining cranberry juice. Stir this mixture into the heated cranberries. Chill until slightly thickened, or for about 30 minutes.
3. Spoon over the baked cheesecake, which has been removed from its pan, then chill again for about 45 minutes.

Serves 8 to 10.

PUOLUKKAPUURO

Cranberries replace Finnish whortleberries in this Scandinavian pudding.

2 cups cranberries
3 cups water
½ cup granulated sugar
1 cup semolina or cream of wheat
½ teaspoon almond extract

1. Boil the berries in the water, uncovered, until they are soft (about 5 minutes). Drain, reserving the juice.
2. Add the sugar to the juice over low heat and gradually add the semolina or cream of wheat. Cook until thickened, about 10 minutes.
3. Mash the berries and mix them into the pudding. Add almond extract. Chill.
4. Just before serving, whip until frothy. Spoon into small dessert dishes and serve with whipped cream.

Serves 4.

POPCORN BALLS CRANBERRY-FLAVORED

Kids enjoy helping with these.

1⅓ cups granulated sugar
1 cup cranberry juice cocktail
2 tablespoons light corn syrup
12 cups popped corn

1. Butter the sides of a heavy 2-quart kettle. Add the sugar, cranberry juice, and syrup. Cook to the hard ball stage (250°F to 268°F).
2. Pour the hot mixture slowly and evenly over the popped corn, stirring enough so it is evenly distributed.
3. Butter your hands and form the popcorn into balls. Cool.
4. Cover each ball in clear plastic wrap and tie each with festive ribbons for jolly stocking stuffers or Christmas giveaways.

Makes about 20.

STUFFED CRANAPPLES JUBILEE

Wrapped in a shiny crust and stuffed with a rich fruit mixture, these apples are a variation on an old recipe from Nova Scotia. Save for a special occasion.

2 tablespoons melted butter
2 tablespoons granulated sugar
1 tablespoon chopped nuts
¼ teaspoon ground cinnamon
2 tablespoons grated orange rind
½ cup chopped cranberries
4 medium cooking apples
1½ tablespoons lemon juice
Pastry dough for an 8- or 9-inch pie crust
1 egg yolk mixed with 1 tablespoon melted butter

1. Preheat the oven to 350°F.
2. Combine the butter, sugar, nuts, cinnamon, orange rind, and cranberries. Set aside.
3. Core the apples and remove a little of their meat so they are well hollowed. Brush the hollows with lemon juice and stuff them with the fruit mixture.
4. Prepare the pastry, rolling it into a large square. Trim it around the edges so it is even and then cut it into 4 squares of the same size. Place an apple on top of each square and brush the pastry with a little water. Bring the corners of each square to the top of its apple and pinch the edges of the pastry together well so the apple is completely covered.
5. Brush each crusted apple with the egg yolk-butter mixture.
6. Put the apples in a shallow pan and bake in the preheated oven for about 40 minutes, or until the apples have baked through and the crust is golden brown, basting once with the juice.
7. Serve warm, with ice cream or whipped cream.

Serves 4.

TOWN HALL CRANBERRY PIE

Warm yourself with this old New England dish that's really a cross between a "betty" and a pie. Easy to make, too.

Filling

1½ cups canned whole cranberry sauce
1½ cups very well drained crushed pineapple
½ teaspoon lemon juice
½ cup chopped walnuts

Crust and Topping

½ cup (1 stick) softened butter
½ cup all-purpose flour
1 cup quick-cooking oats
1 cup light brown sugar

1. Preheat the oven to 325°F.
2. Combine all the filling ingredients and set aside.
3. Mix all the crust and topping ingredients together with your hands. Press half into a 9-inch pie plate, again using your hands to spread the dough evenly onto the bottom and the sides. Set the remainder aside.
4. Pour the cranberry-pineapple mixture over the crust.
5. Spread and flatten the rest of the crust and topping mixture and distribute it over the filling. Don't expect it to cover the filling completely; just drop it in pieces, letting some of the cranberry mixture show through. Bake in the preheated oven for 40 minutes.
6. Serve warm, with vanilla ice cream, if desired.

Serves 8.

CRANBERRY JELLY

New Englanders have long enjoyed this atop slices of brown bread and cream cheese. It also makes a superb topping for French toast.

1 pound cranberries
1 cup water
2¼ cups granulated sugar

1. Boil the berries, covered, in the water for 10 minutes. Put in a jelly bag (see page 11).
2. Add the sugar to the juice and stir once, then let the mixture return to a boil. Remove immediately from the stove.
3. Pour into hot, sterilized half-pint jars and seal according to the directions on page 11.

Makes about 1 pint.

CRANBERRY CHUTNEY

¾ teaspoon whole cloves
3 inches stick cinnamon
2 cups granulated sugar
½ cup distilled white vinegar
1 pound cranberries

1. Tie the cloves and cinnamon in a small cheesecloth bag. Put in a saucepan along with the sugar and vinegar and bring to a boil.
2. Add the cranberries and cook slowly, uncovered, and without stirring, until all the skins have popped open.
3. Remove the spice bag and pour the chutney into hot, sterilized jars. Process in a boiling water bath (page 12) if you plan to store at room temperature or refrigerate or freeze until ready to use.

Makes about 2 pints.

CRANBERRY-BLUEBERRY JAM

Cranberries are high in natural pectin, so commercial pectin need not be added to this flavorful preserve.

1 quart blueberries
1 pound cranberries
6 cups packed light brown sugar
1 tablespoon grated lemon rind

1. Place the fruit in a kettle and crush slightly so the juices begin to run. Mix in the sugar, add the lemon rind, and let the mixture stand overnight, or for at least 6 hours.
2. Heat the fruit and boil, uncovered, until the mixture thickens, about 15 minutes.
3. Pack in hot, sterilized jars and seal (pages 10 and 11).

Makes 2½ pints.

CRANBERRY CONSERVE

1 pound cranberries
1 cup water
1 cup seedless raisins
1 orange, unpeeled, sliced and seeds removed
2½ cups granulated sugar
1 cup chopped nuts

1. Cook the cranberries in the water, uncovered, until all the skins pop.
2. Grind the raisins and the sliced orange in a grinder or blender, then add to the cranberries. Add the sugar and cook for 15 minutes, or until thickened. Add the nuts and remove from the heat.
3. Pack in hot, sterilized glasses and seal (pages 10 and 11).

Makes about 2 pints.

CLASSIC WHOLE CRANBERRY SAUCE

Many people think that homemade cranberry sauce is mysteriously difficult and time consuming to prepare. But it's easy and provides as much noisy fun as popping corn—an activity that it resembles. This recipe is not as thick as commercially canned varieties and serves as a good topping or drizzle for a number of dishes. If drained slightly it could be used in any of the recipes in this book that call for whole cranberry sauce.

2 cups water
1½ cups granulated sugar
1 pound cranberries

1. Boil the water and sugar for 5 minutes in a heavy saucepan, uncovered.
2. Add the berries and boil, uncovered, without stirring until all the skins have popped. You'll be able to hear this—the sound of popping cranberries is as distinctive as that of popping corn. The popping will take about 5 minutes.
3. Let cool and refrigerate.

Makes 5 cups.

Variations: Additions of chopped nuts, cinnamon, ginger, grated orange or lemon peel, and/or a few teaspoons of rum will bring special accents to your own cranberry sauce.

Suggestions for Serving: Place grapefruit sections or sliced peaches or melon in tall stemmed glasses and drizzle the sauce over them for an interesting salad or appetizer. Pass as an accompaniment to poultry, ham, or beef. Or finish a meal by spooning on top of ice cream, sherbet, or pudding.

CRANBERRY-ORANGE RELISH

No cooking at all is necessary for this regal accompaniment to hot and cold meats.

1 pound cranberries
2 oranges
2 cups granulated sugar

1. Put the cranberries through a food chopper. Slice the oranges, remove their seeds, and put the rind and oranges through the chopper.
2. Mix with the berries and sugar, then refrigerate for several hours before serving.

Makes about 2 pints.

GLAZED CRANBERRIES

Oven heat maintains the firmness of the berries while the sugar bathes them in a rosy syrup. Serve this as a complement to chicken or pork in place of cranberry sauce, or simply eat it like candy!

2 cups cranberries
1 cup granulated sugar

1. Preheat the oven to 350°F.
2. Mix the berries with the sugar. Pour into a 9-inch baking pan in a single layer.
3. Bake for 30 minutes; cool for another 30 minutes before serving.

Serves 4.

BURGUNDY BERRY WINE PUNCH

1 pound cranberries
4 cups boiling water
2 cups granulated sugar
1 quart bottle of burgundy wine, chilled
One 6-ounce can frozen orange juice concentrate, defrosted
⅓ cup lemon juice
1 quart bottle sparkling water, chilled

1. Cook the cranberries in the boiling water, uncovered, until the skins pop; strain through a fine sieve.
2. Add the sugar and stir over low heat to dissolve. Chill.
3. At serving time, mix the cranberry juice, wine, orange juice concentrate, and lemon juice in a punch bowl. Add the club soda and a large block of ice and serve.

Fills about 40 punch cups.

NONALCOHOLIC CRANBERRY PUNCH

1 pound cranberries
4 cups water
1⅓ cups granulated sugar
1⅓ cups orange juice
⅔ cup lemon juice
1 cup pineapple juice
3½ cups chilled club soda
Lime sherbet for garnish

1. Combine the cranberries with the water and the sugar and cook them, uncovered, until their skins pop. Strain through a fine sieve. Combine the cranberry juice with the remaining juices and chill.
2. Just before serving, add the club soda and garnish with scoops of lime sherbet.

Fills about 40 punch cups.

Note: If you wish, 1½ quarts of cranberry juice cocktail may be used in place of the cranberry juice made in step 1.

CRANBERRY GLOGG

A hot, spicy drink to serve during wintry frosts. Or pour it into a thermos bottle and warm yourself at a football game.

6 whole cloves
6 inches stick cinnamon
4 whole, shelled cardamom seeds
4 cups cranberry juice cocktail
1 cup light raisins
¼ cup granulated sugar
2 cups port wine

1. Tie the spices in a cheesecloth bag and place in a saucepan. Add 2 cups of the cranberry juice, ¾ cup raisins, and the sugar. Heat to the boiling point, then reduce the heat and let simmer, uncovered, for 10 minutes.
2. Remove the spices and let the punch cool.
3. Just before serving, add the rest of the cranberry juice and the wine. Bring almost to the boiling point, then pour into a heatproof pitcher and serve in mugs or punch cups, sprinkling the remaining raisins into each serving.

Makes about 6 cups.

CRANBERRY TEA

1 pound cranberries
2 oranges, unpeeled, sliced
2 lemons, unpeeled, sliced
3 sticks cinnamon
12 cloves
3½ quarts water
Honey, granulated sugar, or cranberry preserves to taste

1. Combine all the ingredients except the sweetener and bring to a boil. Let simmer, uncovered, for 40 minutes.
2. Strain and serve hot, sweetened to taste with honey, sugar, or cranberry preserves.

Makes 10 to 12 cups.

CUR-RANTS

Elf, will you sell me your berries bright
For to make me a pot of jam?
—From "Elfin Berries"
by RACHEL FIELD

Currants are to food what dry wit is to conversation. They add verve, zest, and interest while their very presence in a dish prevents it from being blandly sweet or overly sentimental.

Red, black or white—they grow on low bushes, glistening under the summer sun like small beads waiting to be strung on a necklace. The white ones are so transparent that you can actually see the seeds inside. Don't let their absence of color prevent you from using them, however. They have a delicate flavor, and when prepared for jelly, they take on a pearly sheen which makes an intriguing and lovely spread for toast, and whole-wheat and brown bread.

Currants belong to the gooseberry family, requiring similar soil and cultivation. Where you'll find one, you'll often find the other; produce farms frequently grow currant bushes on acreage adjacent to the gooseberry crop. But these tartly flavored berries are only cultivated in this country to a small extent. Currants may be found wild in many places, though, especially on the West Coast. Preceded by clusters of showy red flowers which color the spring landscape, they are particularly rich in vitamin C and natural pectin. Europeans are fond of combining them with raspberries, and the French have elevated currants to their chief culinary fame in the form of Bar-le-Duc, a tart and elegant jelly which enhances meat sauces and glazes.

If you were ever to watch a "Name's the Same" Berry Show, you would see two different types of fruit rise to claim the name of "currant": the red, black and white kind featured in this chapter; and a dried, shriveled, seedless type that resembles a small raisin. The fact is that the label "currant" describes two separate varieties of fruit, and both of them have separate uses in the kitchen. Dried currants derive their name from their ancient origins in Corinth and are packaged and prepared like raisins; currants from the *Ribes* family are cooked fresh in ways that the following recipes will show.

SANJIT'S CURRANT RICE CURRY

Sanjit serves this pungent dish as the main course of a vegetarian meal, accompanied by fresh bread and herbal tea.

¼ cup oil
2 large sweet onions, minced
2 cups tomato puree
1 tablespoon lemon juice
2 tablespoons brown sugar
1 teaspoon curry powder or to taste
2 tablespoons water
1 cup fresh red currants
3 tart apples, cored and chopped (unpeeled)
½ cup shredded coconut
½ cup chopped, fresh parsley
4 cups brown rice

1. Heat the oil in a skillet; add onions and sauté until soft. Add the tomato puree, lemon juice and brown sugar; bring to a boil.
2. Mix curry powder with water and stir into onion mixture. Cook over medium heat, uncovered, for 2 minutes.
3. Add currants, apples, coconut and parsley; cook for several minutes, until just heated through. Serve warm over brown rice.

Serves 4.

PETITE RED CURRANT MOLDS

Tartness and color make these piquant accompaniments for meat or fowl.

3 cups fresh red currants
1 tablespoon granulated sugar
½ cup orange juice
½ cup water
One 3-ounce package raspberry gelatin
1 tablespoon grated orange rind
Sour cream or plain yogurt for garnish

1. Cook 2 cups of the currants with the sugar, orange juice, and water over medium heat in a small saucepan, stirring frequently until the skins pop.
2. Force through a sieve. Add the gelatin to the liquid fruit mixture, as well as the grated orange rind. Refrigerate until partially thickened.
3. Fold the remaining 1 cup of currants into the gelatin mixture. Pour into small, individual molds and chill until firm.
4. Unmold, top with sour cream or yogurt, and serve.

Serves 4.

CURRANT-CARROT MUFFINS

½ cup dry milk powder
3 teaspoons baking powder
¼ teaspoon salt
½ teaspoon allspice
1 teaspoon cinnamon
2½ cups whole-wheat flour
1 cup honey
1 cup oil
4 eggs
1 teaspoon vanilla extract
1 cup fresh red or black currants
1 cup grated carrots

1. Preheat the oven to 400°F. Grease two muffin tins.
2. Combine the dry milk powder, baking powder, salt, spices and whole-wheat flour. In a separate bowl, mix the honey, oil, eggs, and vanilla extract; stir mixture into the dry ingredients, mixing until well blended. Fold in the currants and carrots.
3. Fill the greased muffin tins about two-thirds full and bake in the preheated oven for 15 to 20 minutes, or until done.

Makes 2 dozen.

KRISTEN'S TRIFLE

One 3-ounce package vanilla pudding mix
2 cups heavy cream
½ cup whipping cream
1½ cups cubed pound cake (about 2 slices)
1 tablespoon fruit-flavored liqueur
½ cup red currant jelly
1 cup raspberries
½ cup fresh mint leaves

1. Prepare the pudding mix as directed on the package, using 2 cups heavy cream instead of milk. Cover with waxed paper and let cool until lukewarm.
2. Whip the ½ cup whipping cream; fold gently into the pudding.
3. Place the cake cubes in a glass bowl and drizzle them with the liqueur. Cover evenly with the currant jelly.
4. Add ¾ cup of the raspberries; cover with the pudding, using a rubber spatula to spread it evenly over all.
5. Arrange the remaining raspberries around the edge of the pudding, placing one in the very middle. Tuck the mint leaves in among the circle of berries. Cover and refrigerate until well set, at least 6 hours.

Serves 4.

SCANDINAVIAN FRUIT PUDDING

This is so popular in Denmark that it is sometimes referred to as "the Danish national pudding." The Danes make it distinctive by arranging almonds in a star-shaped pattern over the top. Known as *rodgrod* in Scandinavia, similarly prepared dishes in the United States are often called "flummeries."

1 pint red currants
1 pint red raspberries
2 cups water
1 cup granulated sugar
¼ teaspoon salt
⅓ cup cornstarch
1 tablespoon lemon juice
⅓ cup blanched almonds, split in half

1. Place the fruits in a large saucepan with 1½ cups of the water. Cover and let simmer for 10 minutes.
2. Strain through a fine sieve; discard the pulp. Measure the juice into another pan and add water, if necessary, to make 2½ cups liquid. Add the sugar and salt and heat to boiling, stirring all the while.
3. Mix the cornstarch with the remaining ½ cup water and stir it into the fruit juice. Bring back to a boil and cook for 3 minutes, again stirring all the while.
4. Remove from heat and blend in lemon juice, then pour the mixture into a glass bowl. Decorate the top by arranging the almonds in a star-shaped pattern.
5. Chill before serving.

Serves 4.

CURRANT-ALMOND COFFEE CAKE

3 cups all-purpose flour (unsifted)
2 teaspoons baking powder
1 teaspoon ground cinnamon
½ teaspoon ground allspice
¼ teaspoon salt
1 cup (2 sticks) butter or margarine
2 cups granulated sugar
4 eggs
1 cup sour cream
2 cups black currants
1 cup slivered or chopped almonds

1. Preheat the oven to 325°F. Grease and flour a 10-inch tube pan.
2. Combine the flour, baking powder, cinnamon, allspice, and salt. Set aside.
3. In a separate bowl cream together the butter or margarine and sugar. Add the eggs, one at a time, beating well after each addition. Add half of the flour mixture, all of the sour cream, and then the remaining flour, beating well after each addition. Fold in the currants and nuts.
4. Bake in the preheated oven for 1½ hours, or until the cake tests done.
5. Cool the cake for 10 minutes before removing from the pan, then invert onto a wire rack until cool.

Serves 8 to 10.

CURRANT JELLY, AMERICAN STYLE

Strained in the standard way, this jelly completely eliminates the crunchy seeds found in currants.

2 quarts currants (red, black, or white)
½ cup water
One 1¾-ounce box powdered pectin
5 cups sugar

1. Mash the currants in a preserving kettle. Add ½ cup water and bring to a slow boil. Let boil for a few minutes until the currants become soft. Strain through cheesecloth that has been placed in a colander or in a jelly bag.
2. Return juices to the kettle and add the powdered pectin. Stir over high heat until the mixture is brought to a rolling boil. Add sugar. Continue boiling for 1 minute, stirring all the while.
3. Remove from heat and skim off the foam with a metal spoon. Pour into hot, sterilized jars and seal (pages 10 and 11).

Makes 2½ pints.

BAR-LE-DUC

This beautiful and classic French jelly is often used in sauces to accompany meat or fowl.

4 cups red currants
3 cups granulated sugar

1. Wash and stem the currants. Cook them in a flat pan with a small amount of water to prevent sticking. Let simmer, uncovered, for 5 minutes.
2. Add 1½ cups of the sugar. Stir gently and let boil, uncovered, for 5 minutes, then add the remaining sugar, and boil rapidly for 5 more minutes. Let stand until cool.
3. Skim out the currants with a slotted spoon and ladle into hot, sterilized half-pint jars. Boil the syrup to the jellying point (page 11), then pour, while hot, over the currants. Seal immediately (see page 11).

Makes 3 half-pints.

BLACK CURRANT JAM

Carol Makielski of Makielski's Berry Farm in Ypsilanti, Michigan, especially likes this jam because, without cooking, its high vitamin C content remains intact.

1½ quarts black currants
½ cup orange juice
¾ cup water
1¾-ounce box of powdered pectin
5 cups sugar

1. Place the currants and juice in a blender and whirl to chop the currants. Stir in sugar. Pour this mixture into a bowl and let it stand for 10 minutes.
2. Mix the water with the pectin in a saucepan and bring to a boil. Boil for 1 minute, stirring continually. Pour the pectin solution into the fruit mixture and stir for 2 minutes.
3. Pour the jam into sterilized jars and seal (see page 11). Let jam set at room temperature for 24 hours before storing it in the freezer.

Makes 4 pints.

CURRANT SAUCE

½ cup finely shredded orange peel
3 tablespoons finely shredded lemon peel
1½ cups orange juice
½ cup lemon juice
2 cups currant jelly
1 cup Madeira wine
2 teaspoons dry mustard
1 teaspoon ground ginger
½ teaspoon salt
½ teaspoon red pepper sauce

1. In a small saucepan combine the orange and lemon peel and the juices. Bring to a boil, then cook over medium heat, uncovered, for 20 minutes, or until the peel becomes translucent.
2. Add the jelly, wine, mustard, ginger, salt, and red pepper sauce. Bring to a boil, stirring constantly, then reduce the heat and simmer, uncovered, for 30 minutes, or until the sauce is reduced to 2½ cups.
3. Cool for 10 minutes, then serve as an accompaniment to Cornish game hen or other poultry.

Makes 2½ cups.

CURRANT-RASPBERRY SOUP

The combination of these two berries has delighted Europeans for many years. Here they are found in a Polish soup that is traditionally served as the last course of a meal.

1 pint red or black raspberries
1 pint red or black currants
4 cups boiling water
1 teaspoon cornstarch
2 tablespoons cold water
½ cup granulated sugar
⅔ cup sour cream

1. Crush the berries through a sieve; save the juice. Add the berry pulp to the boiling water and let simmer, uncovered, for 15 minutes.
2. Strain through a sieve, then return to the saucepan. Add the cornstarch, mixed with the 2 tablespoons cold water.
3. Bring to a boil, then stir in the sugar and chill thoroughly.
4. Just before serving, add the reserved juice, which has been mixed with the sour cream.

Serves 6.

Note: Nut Dumplings (page 15) are a tasty accompaniment to this soup.

CASSIS

Currants add intrigue to this liqueur, which is often drunk in France with the delightful addition of white wine.

1 quart brandy
3 cups black currants
1½ teaspoons ground cloves
2 sticks cinnamon
2 cups granulated sugar

1. Place the brandy, currants, cloves, and cinnamon in a stone jar. Cover well and let stand for 2 months in a cool, dark place.
2. Strain and add sugar. Stir well until the sugar dissolves. Bottle. Store in a cool, dark place.

Makes 2 pints.

COPENHAGEN PUNCH BOWL

Here is a liquid version of the Scandinavian Fruit Pudding.

1 cup currant juice
1 cup raspberry juice
2 lemons, sliced thin
1 orange, peeled and sliced
1 pineapple, peeled and cut into small chunks
½ cup blanched almonds, split in half
5 tablespoons granulated sugar, or to taste
1 quart club soda
1½ trays ice

1. Pour the juices into a bowl. Add the lemon and orange slices, then the pineapple chunks. Mix in the halved almonds and the sugar; the mixture should be moderately sweet.
2. Cover the bowl and let refrigerate overnight.
3. Just before serving, add the club soda and ice.

Fills 20 punch cups.

Note: To make currant or raspberry juice, place 1 quart of currants or raspberries in a pot and add 1 tablespoon of water. Cook over medium heat until the berries are soft (about 10 minutes). Strain through a jelly bag or several layers of cheesecloth.

ELDER-BERRIES

But I can't help thinkin' about the time
You were a wife of mine;
You aimed to please me, cooked black-eyed peas-me,
Made Elderberry Wine.

Drunk all the time, feelin' fine
On Elderberry Wine,
Those were the days, we'd lie in the haze
Forget depressive times.

—From the song "Elderberry Wine"
(lyrics by BERNIE TAUPIN,
music by ELTON JOHN)

The grandfather of all berries is the elderberry, which grows plentifully in large, dark clusters on the branches of the tree whose name it bears. For thousands of years its leaves were used to make a tea that soothed stomach disorders, and the Indians used its powerful bark in small, careful doses as a natural cathartic. So benevolent and widespread were its healing powers that a famous physician is said to have raised his hat in reverence to the elder tree every time he passed one by.

Elderberries grow wild throughout the country, along roadsides, railroads, and on the edges of wooded areas. Rarely are they cultivated or grown commercially; if you want them you'll most likely have to carry a basket and search for them yourself. Learn to recognize the flower of the elder tree, which blossoms in the springtime in a series of clusters, or umbels, so you can return in the late summer or early autumn to pick the berries that will appear in the same grouped pattern.

Elder flowers, white and lacy in appearance, are about 4 to 6 inches in diameter and may be eaten themselves in a number of ways. They have a delightfully delicate taste, and when heated in water create a flowery aroma that will subtly perfume your entire kitchen.

The berries themselves are deep purple to black and contain rich concentrations of vitamin C. (Stay away from the red elderberry, *S. pubens*, which is poisonous.) Edible elderberries are pea-sized or even smaller, but fortunately they can be quickly picked, for hundreds of them will be found on one umbel. Like most wild berries they have a tongue-teasing tartness that is welcome in jams, jellies, and other foods.

It is sad but true that most people have never tasted either the fruit or the flower of the elder, although these were not uncommon in the diets of bygone days. Perhaps, as people have moved further away from the land, they forgot about the elder, its berry and its flower, and are thus bypassing one of nature's most benevolent and plentiful gifts.

Here are but a few elder recipes that were often served with pride in old-fashioned parlors. You can serve them, too, as unexpected and nostalgic treats for all ages.

ELDERBERRY ZABAGLIONE

4 egg yolks
¼ cup granulated sugar
½ cup Marsala wine
2 tablespoons dry sherry
1 cup elderberries

1. Combine the first 4 ingredients in a large, flat-bottomed stainless steel or copper bowl that has been set over very hot water. Beat until frothy.
2. Continue beating until the mixture thickens. Remove from the heat and fold in the berries.
3. Pour immediately into long-stemmed wine glasses and serve.

Serves 4.

ELDERBERRY-APPLE PIE

Tart elderberries combine well with apples in both taste and appearance. Use this recipe when you are able to obtain only a limited number of elderberries.

4 cups sliced, peeled apples
1 cup elderberries
¾ teaspoon ground cinnamon
2 tablespoons all-purpose flour
1 tablespoon lemon juice
Pastry for a Two-Crust Pie (page 20)
1 tablespoon butter

1. Preheat the oven to 375°F.
2. Combine the apples, berries, cinnamon, flour, and lemon juice.
3. Roll out half the pastry and fit into an 8-inch pie pan. Put in the filling mixture and dot with the butter.
4. Roll out the remaining pastry and place over the filling. Seal, flute, and cut slits in the center. Cover the edges of the crust with a 1½-inch strip of aluminum foil to prevent overbrowning.
5. Bake in the preheated oven for 35 to 40 minutes, or until the crust is browned and the filling is bubbling.

Serves 8.

ELDERBERRY JELLY

3 pounds elderberries
½ cup lemon juice
6 cups granulated sugar
One 6-ounce bottle liquid pectin

1. Remove the major stems from the berries, then place in a preserving kettle and crush. Heat over a moderate flame for about 5 minutes, or until the juices begin to flow.
2. Strain through a jelly bag (see page 11) until you have 3 cups of juice. Return to the preserving kettle.
3. Add the lemon juice and sugar to the berry juice. Bring to a boil until the sugar dissolves.
4. Add the liquid pectin, then bring to a boil and boil for 1 minute, stirring constantly. Skim off the foam and pour into hot, sterilized jars or jelly glasses. Seal (see page 11).

Makes about 3 pints.

ELDERBERRY-APPLE JELLY

The natural pectin in the apples eliminates the need for commercial pectin.

2 quarts ripe elderberries
4 medium cooking apples
2 quarts water
Granulated sugar
1 tablespoon orange juice

1. Remove the major stems from the berries. Crush berries, then place in a preserving kettle.
2. Cut the apples into slices and add them to the berries. Mash the mixture, add water, and let simmer, uncovered, for 20 minutes. Stir frequently to prevent the mixture from sticking to the bottom.
3. Strain the fruits through a jelly bag (page 11), then measure the juice and return to the preserving kettle. Add 1 cup of granulated sugar for each cup of juice. Add the orange juice and bring to a boil for 1 minute.
4. Lower the heat and cook, uncovered, until the liquid falls away from a metal spoon in sheets rather than in drops. Pour into hot, sterilized jars and seal (see page 11).

Makes about 2½ pints.

ELDERBERRY CATSUP

5 cups elderberries
2½ cups cider vinegar
1¼ cups granulated sugar
1 tablespoon lemon juice
½ teaspoon ground ginger
½ teaspoon ground cinnamon
2 teaspoons ground cloves
1 tablespoon ground allspice
⅛ teaspoon cayenne pepper

1. Combine the berries and vinegar in a large saucepan and boil gently, uncovered, until the berries become soft (no longer than 10 minutes).
2. Press through a sieve to remove the skins and seeds, then return to the saucepan and add the remaining ingredients.
3. Bring to a boil and let boil, uncovered, for 10 minutes. Pour into hot, sterilized jars and seal. Process in a boiling water bath (page 12).

Makes 2½ pints.

ELDERBERRY WINE

Famous for its healing qualities, the elder produces that most benevolent healer of all—wine.

4 pounds ripe elderberries
5 quarts water
3 pounds granulated sugar
8 ounces raisins, chopped
1 cake compressed yeast, mashed with a fork until liquefied and spread on a slice of toast

1. Remove the major stems from the berries and put the berries in a large stock pot with the water. Bring to a boil and boil for 10 minutes.
2. Strain through a jelly bag (page 11) and return the liquid to the stock pot. Add the sugar to the liquid, as well as the chopped raisins. Simmer for 20 minutes, then let cool.
3. Add the yeast spread on toast and leave to ferment for 3 weeks.
4. Skim and strain into a stone jar. Cork loosely until fermentation ceases.
5. Tighten the cork. The wine will keep for 6 to 9 months.

Makes about a gallon.

ELDER FLOWER FRITTERS

Celebrate the coming of spring by serving these flower-shaped hot morsels.

1 cup sifted all-purpose flour
2 tablespoons melted butter
1 tablespoon Cognac
1 cup lukewarm water
Vegetable oil for deep frying
3 egg whites, at room temperature
12 perfect, large, ripe elder flower clusters, picked with 1 inch of stalk
1 cup confectioners' sugar

1. Put the flour into a bowl and make a well in the middle. Add the butter, Cognac, and water to the well and gradually combine with the flour until the mixture is smooth. Let stand, covered, for 1 hour.
2. While the batter is standing, fill a deep fryer ¾ full with vegetable oil and heat oil to 375°F.
3. Beat the egg whites into firm peaks and fold into the batter. Dip the flowers into this mixture and fry in the hot oil, with stems up. When golden brown (about 1 or 2 minutes), lift out by the stem, using a long-handled prong, and let drain on absorbent paper.
4. Coat with confectioners' sugar and serve at once.

Serves 6, with 2 clusters to each plate.

ELDER FLOWER SHERBET

A light but distinctive way to top off a heavy meal.

2 cups water
4 cups elder flowers
½ cup granulated sugar
1 egg white
½ cup heavy cream
1 tablespoon orange juice

1. Combine the water and flowers and simmer gently, uncovered, for 10 minutes.

2. Discard the flowers and add the sugar to the liquid. Let simmer, still uncovered, for 10 minutes, then set aside to cool.
3. Beat the egg white until stiff. In a separate bowl, beat the cream until thick. Fold the egg white into the cream, then fold the mixture into the cooled sugar-flower syrup.
4. Blend in the orange juice, then pour into an ice tray. Freeze until barely frozen. Beat the mixture until it becomes fluffy. Freeze again until firm.

Serves 4.

ELDER FLOWERADE

A delicately flavored drink with a taste somewhere between lemonade and a light wine.

8 clusters freshly picked elder flowers
2 quarts cold water
1 lemon
1 tablespoon malt or cider vinegar
1½ cups granulated sugar

1. Cover the elder flowers with the cold water. Add the lemon, sliced into quarters, the malt or cider vinegar, and the sugar. Stir well. Let stand, covered, for 24 hours, stirring occasionally.
2. Strain the mixture into a large pan and simmer the liquid for 15 minutes. Store, refrigerated, in a covered ceramic bowl or stone crock for 1 week before serving.

Makes 2 quarts.

Ribes

GOOSE-BERRIES

The young folks of Northamptonshire, after eating as much as they possibly can of this gooseberry fool, are said frequently to roll down a hill and begin eating again.

—From KETTNER's *Book of the Table* (1877)

Gooseberries enjoy their greatest popularity in Europe, especially in Great Britain, where they have thrived in English gardens since the reign of Henry VIII. Shows dedicated to presentations of ever larger and more stupendous gooseberries are held throughout England; the Old Gooseberry Society of Yorkshire, for example, was founded in 1800 and still holds its annual competition on the first Tuesday in August of each year. In 1952 a now-legendary berry weighing nearly two ounces was the star and record-breaking attraction.

First cousins to currants, gooseberries were first brought to the United States in the sixteenth century by colonists who had a traditional hankering to eat them in pies during the festival of Whitsuntide, just as they had back in England.

Today gooseberries are grown on a small scale in North America. The commonest variety is pale green with rather transparent skin, revealing amusing little stripes or "veins." These taste and look much like tart green grapes, except that they come with two stemlike appendages on each end, which makes it necessary that you "top and tail" them before using. Lesser-known types of gooseberries may be red or yellow.

Surprisingly enough, canned gooseberries are sometimes available on American supermarket shelves.

One 16-ounce can gooseberries = 2 cups gooseberries in syrup

GOOSEBERRY FOOL

The fool, a delightfully named dessert that dates back to sixteenth-century England, is a variation of simple fruit and cream in which pureed fruit creates swirls of color as it circles throughout stiffened mounds of whipped cream. To most effectively show off your fool, you should serve it in a glass bowl so its colors may be properly appreciated.

Not traditional here is the addition of cream cheese, which, I feel, adds extra body and richness.

If you are unable to find gooseberries for this "foolish" treat, try using kiwi fruit, commonly but erroneously known as "Chinese gooseberries." Available in many specialty shops, they are not true gooseberries at all, but their color and tartness enable them to be tasty substitutes. The meat of 12 kiwi fruits may be used in place of 1 pint of gooseberries. Blackberries, blueberries, and raspberries may also be substituted.

1 pint of gooseberries
½ cup granulated sugar, or to taste
1½ teaspoons cornstarch
One 3-ounce package cream cheese
¼ cup confectioners' sugar
1 teaspoon vanilla extract
1 cup heavy cream
1 teaspoon grated lemon rind

1. Place the berries in a medium-sized saucepan, mix in the sugar and cornstarch, and cook, uncovered, over medium heat, stirring often. Crush a few berries, if necessary, until the mixture thickens slightly, and let bubble for 1 minute.
2. Remove from the heat. Put through a sieve and refrigerate the pureed berries until cold.
3. Beat the cream cheese until it is soft; blend in the confectioners' sugar and vanilla. Add the cream and beat until fluffy and soft peaks form.
4. Spoon the creamy mixture over the pureed berries, and then, very gently, fold it in until the puree is swirled throughout the cream.
5. Sprinkle with the lemon rind, and refrigerate until ready to serve.

Serves 4.

GOOSEBERRY SOUFFLE WITH VANILLA SAUCE

In Scandinavian countries, gooseberries may come to the table prepared like this.

2 eggs, separated
1 tablespoon cornstarch
2 tablespoons grated lemon peel
¼ cup dry white wine
4 cups gooseberries
3 tablespoons water
1 teaspoon lemon juice
2½ tablespoons sugar
Vanilla Sauce (below)

1. Preheat the oven to 375°F. Grease a 1-quart soufflé dish or ovenproof casserole.
2. Mix the egg yolks and cornstarch with the lemon peel and white wine. Set aside.
3. Simmer the berries, uncovered, with the water, lemon juice, and sugar until tender (about 5 minutes). Sieve. Pour a little puree into the yolk mixture and then mix altogether into the rest of the puree. Let cool.
4. Beat the egg whites until stiff, then fold into the lemon sauce.
5. Pour the soufflé mixture into the prepared dish and bake in the preheated oven for 30 minutes.
6. Serve immediately. Pass the Vanilla Sauce separately.

Serves 4.

VANILLA SAUCE

1 cup milk
2 egg yolks
1 tablespoon granulaed sugar
½ teaspoon vanilla extract
¼ cup heavy cream

1. Put the milk, egg yolks, sugar, and vanilla in the top of a double boiler and cook over simmering water, stirring constantly, until thickened.
2. Whip the cream, fold it into the egg yolk mixture, and serve.

Makes about 1½ cups.

VIOLET'S GOOSEBERRY MERINGUE PIE

This tastes amazingly like a lemon meringue pie. Use a pastry crust or make a crumb crust. Many people like their gooseberries on top of a chocolate-flavored crumb crust.

3 cups gooseberries
1¼ cups granulated sugar
¼ cup water
1½ tablespoons cornstarch
2 eggs, separated
1 baked 9-inch pie shell (see Pie Crust for Berry Desserts, page 55)

1. Stew the berries gently with 1 cup of the sugar and the water in an uncovered saucepan until tender (about 10 minutes). Put the mixture through a sieve and let cool.
2. Mix the cornstarch with a little of the cooled puree. Heat the rest of the puree in a saucepan, then add the cornstarch mixture. Heat until boiling, stirring constantly. Let boil, uncovered, for 3 minutes.
3. Remove the mixture from the heat. Beat the egg yolks and add to the saucepan, then return to the heat and cook slowly for 4 more minutes. Pour into the baked pie shell and let cool.
4. While the filling is cooling, preheat the oven to 375°F.
5. Beat the egg whites until soft peaks form. Gradually add the remaining ¼ cup sugar and beat until stiff.
6. Pipe the meringue in a lattice design on top of the cooled pie. Bake in the preheated oven for 10 minutes, or until delicately browned.
7. Serve hot or cold.

Serves 8.

GOOSEBERRY PRESERVES

1 quart gooseberries
2 tablespoons lemon juice
⅓ cup water
1 teaspoon grated lemon rind
3 cups granulated sugar
Pinch each of freshly grated nutmeg and ground ginger

1. Place all the ingredients in a kettle and boil, uncovered, until thickened (about 10 minutes).
2. Pack into hot jars and seal (page 11).

Makes about 2 pints.

GOOSEBERRY RELISH

The spices give this a warm, reddish-brown color, while the gooseberries impart their unique tang. Excellent with meats and poultry.

3 cups gooseberries
½ cup dried currants
1½ cups finely chopped onion
¾ cup packed brown sugar
½ teaspoon dry mustard
1 teaspoon ground ginger
1 teaspoon salt
¼ teaspoon cayenne pepper
½ teaspoon turmeric
1 cup vinegar

1. Place all the ingredients in a large pan. Bring to a boil and then let simmer, uncovered, for 45 minutes.
2. Bottle and seal and process in a hot water bath (page 12) or refrigerate until ready to use.

Makes 2½ cups.

MAGYAR GOOSEBERRY SAUCE

The international gooseberry is served in Hungary with the characteristic addition of sour cream. This goes especially well with chicken or turkey.

1 pint gooseberries
2 tablespoons butter
2 tablespoons all-purpose flour
2 egg yolks
¼ teaspoon salt
½ cup granulated sugar
¼ cup chicken broth
½ cup sour cream

1. Cook the gooseberries in the butter, stirring constantly, until softened slightly (about 5 minutes).
2. Blend the flour, egg yolks, salt, and sugar with the chicken broth. Stir into the gooseberries and cook until thickened.
3. Just before serving, mix in the sour cream.

Makes about 3 cups.

GOOSEBERRY SAUCE FOR MACKEREL

Gooseberries in France are called *groseilles à maquereau* or "mackerel gooseberries," due to the great popularity of this dish, regarded by many as a gourmet's delight.

3 cups gooseberries
½ cup granulated sugar
¼ cup (½ stick) butter
2 teaspoons all-purpose flour
½ cup dry white wine
Coarse salt and freshly ground white pepper to taste
Pinch each of freshly grated nutmeg and ground ginger

1. Cover the gooseberries with water, then add the sugar and heat, uncovered, until the berries are softened (about 5 minutes). Put through a sieve and set aside.
2. Melt the butter in a saucepan. Add the flour, stir, and cook for 1 minute. Bring the wine to a boil in a separate pan. Add all at once to the butter-flour mixture, stirring constantly until thickened.
3. Add the pureed gooseberries, salt, pepper, and a touch of nutmeg and ginger, and heat together.
4. Serve warm, as an accompaniment to broiled fish.

Makes about 2 cups.

JUNIPER BERRIES

Lay there by the juniper
While the moon is bright,
Watch the jugs a-fillin'
In the pale moonlight.

—From the song
"The Copper Kettle"
words and music
by ALBERT F. BEDDOE

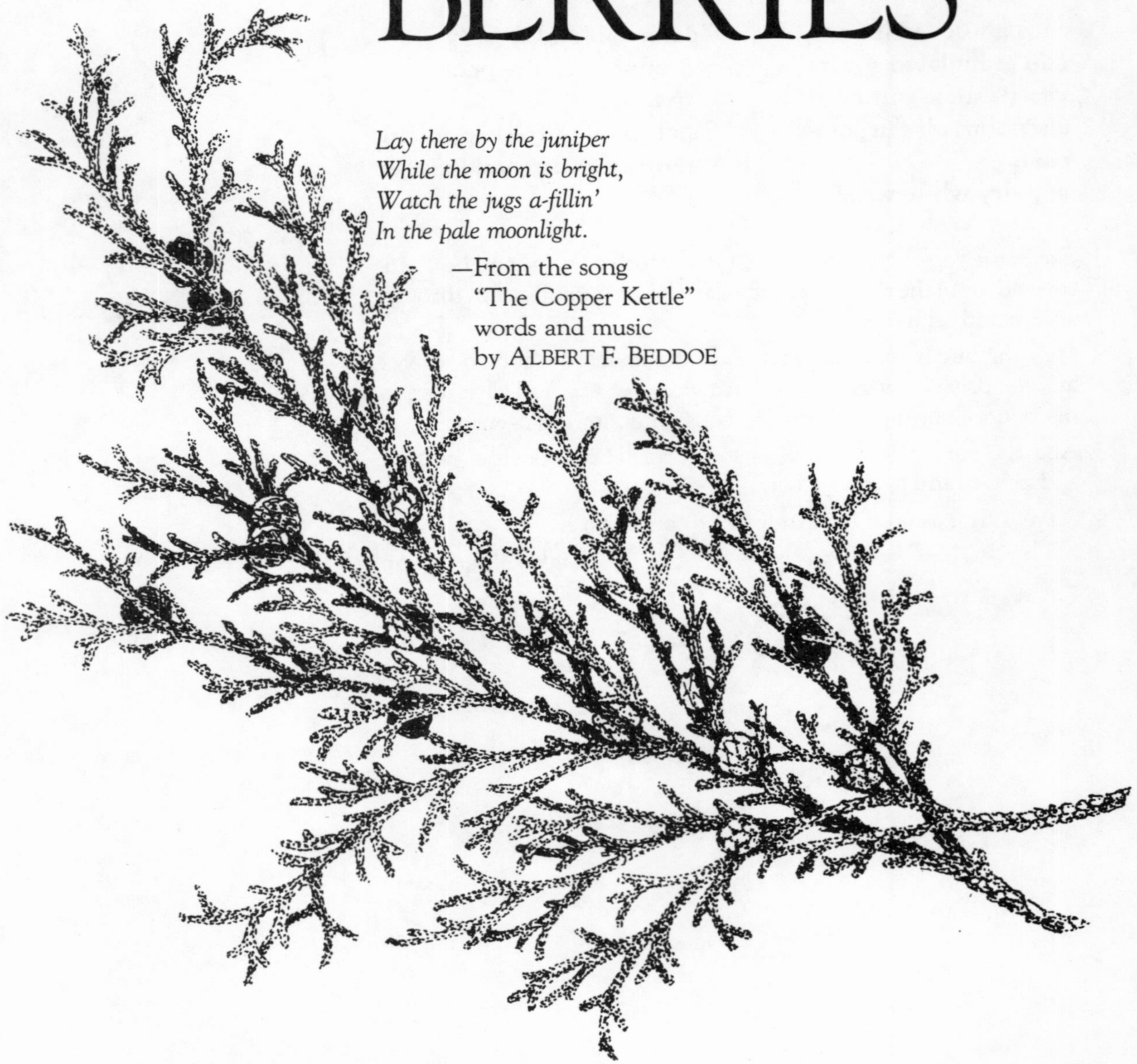

The fruits of the juniper are the spices of the berry world. Like cloves, they are counted one by one as they are added to food because it takes only a few to impart a strong, woodsy flavor to whatever recipe they are chosen to enhance.

The durability of the juniper makes it a favorite garden shrub, one that is commonly sold in many nurseries. If you look around you, you will notice it by many front doors and along houses and buildings as part of the landscaping.

In the ancient past, junipers were regarded as having divine powers. The Bible tells how Elijah the Prophet made a day's journey into the wilderness to escape from King Ahab's revenge: it was under a juniper that he ultimately took shelter and in an anguished state of mind prayed for his own death.

But it was not to be. "As he lay and slept under a juniper tree, behold then an angel touched him, and said unto him, Arise and eat." A freshly baked cake lay by his side.

Cottagers of old burned juniper wood on their hearths to ward off evil spirits, and the berries were used on funeral pyres to protect departing spirits.

Juniper berries are dark blue, and when fully ripe are covered by a faint, frosty bloom. Their unique outdoorsy flavor is an ideal addition to such hearty foods as venison, cabbage, and sauerkraut. The English once used them as a substitute for pepper, and the renowned Limerick ham of Ireland is smoked over juniper berries and branches. Country people have long used them in the flavoring of homemade gin.

Dried juniper berries are available in the spice section of many specialty stores and some supermarkets. Since a 1⁵⁄₁₆-ounce jar contains ½ cup of dried berries, you will be well supplied with this sparingly used flavoring for a very long time.

MARINATED VENISON IN ORANGE SAUCE

Juniper berries meet venison in this rich Scottish recipe.

1½ to 2 pounds haunch of venison
2 cups dry red wine
1 tablespoon cooking oil
2 onions, sliced
1 bay leaf
4 large black peppercorns
6 juniper berries
4 sprigs fresh parsley
2 tablespoons butter, one generous
1 carrot, peeled and sliced
4 stalks celery trimmed and sliced
Grated peel and juice of 1 orange
1 cup beef broth
1 tablespoon cranberry jelly
1 teaspoon salt
1 heaping tablespoon all-purpose flour

1. Tie the meat and put into a deep dish.
2. Make a marinade by combining the wine, oil, 1 sliced onion, bay leaf, peppercorns, juniper berries, and parsley. Bring to the boiling point in a small saucepan, then pour over the meat and marinate, covered, for 24 to 48 hours in the refrigerator so that the flavors may permeate. Turn the meat several times.
3. Preheat the oven to 325°F.
4. Drain the venison, reserving and straining the marinade, then brown on all sides in 1 tablespoon butter in a large flameproof casserole. Remove the meat and add the other onion, carrot, celery, and orange peel. Cook gently for 5 minutes, until the onion becomes soft.
5. Add the beef broth, jelly, orange juice, salt, and the strained marinade juice.
6. Place the meat on top of the vegetables and sauce. Cover the casserole and let bake slowly for 1½ hours, or until the meat is tender.
7. When ready to serve, remove the venison and the vegetables to a warm platter. Strain the liquid.
8. Melt the generous tablespoon of butter in a small saucepan and mix in the flour with a rubber spatula. Add this to the hot meat sauce in order to thicken it and pour into a gravy dish. Serve with the meat and vegetables.

Serves 4.

JUNIPER-FLAVORED STUFFED CABBAGE

8 large cabbage leaves
¾ pound ground beef
1 egg, beaten
1 small onion, finely minced
1 teaspoon salt
One 28-ounce can stewed tomatoes, undrained
1 beef bouillon cube
2 tablespoons brown sugar
8 juniper berries, crushed

1. Pour boiling water over the cabbage leaves and let soak for 10 minutes. Drain well on absorbent paper.
2. Brown the meat and drain. Mix in the egg, onion, and salt, then place in heaping tablespoons on each leaf. Tuck in the sides of each leaf, then carefully roll up, fastening each with toothpicks.
3. Place the stuffed cabbage rolls in a pan. Heat and combine the tomatoes, bouillon cube, brown sugar, and juniper berries. Pour mixture over the cabbage rolls.
4. Cover and bring to a boil, then lower the heat and let simmer for 20 minutes, or until the cabbage is tender.

Serves 4.

JUNIPER-STEAMED VEGETABLES

To impart a unique evergreen flavor and aroma to cabbage or other vegetables, do as the Norwegians do. Pick finger-thick branches of juniper and remove their needles. Arrange them in a grid of several layers in the bottom of a pot and add enough water to fill it halfway up the grid. Place your vegetables on top of this and let them steam until they are done.

SAUERKRAUT WITH JUNIPER BERRIES

2 large onions, diced
1 tablespoon butter
1 tablespoon all-purpose flour
One 28-ounce can sauerkraut
One 10½-ounce can condensed tomato soup
2 teaspoons paprika
2 tablespoons granulated sugar
2 cups water
4 to 6 juniper berries, crushed

1. Brown the onions in butter in a large saucepan. Add the flour and stir until smooth.
2. Add the remaining ingredients to the saucepan, cover, and simmer slowly for 1 hour.

Serves 4.

EVERGREEN TEA

American Indians used the sprigs of the juniper to provide this bracing and invigorating tea.

10 juniper sprigs
5 cups water

1. Wash the juniper sprigs and add them to the water. Bring to a boil and then let simmer for 15 minutes.
2. Strain and serve.

Makes 4 cups.

MULBERRIES

Here we go round the mulberry bush,
The mulberry bush, the mulberry bush,
Here we go round the mulberry bush
So early in the morning!
—Old Nursery Rhyme

It is on the leaves of the white mulberry that silkworms feed, and the plant was grown with great success and profit in the Orient. About 150 years ago it was brought to America in high hopes that a flourishing silk industry would develop around it. Alas, nearly all of the plants died from the cold northern climate, and with them all the plans that had been made for American-grown silk.

Red and black mulberries, which are sturdier, thrive better on American and European soil. Perhaps they even inspire literary creativity. Both William Shakespeare and John Milton had mulberry trees growing near their front doors, and the Milton mulberry is reputed to bear fruit to this very day.

Mild and sweet-flavored, mulberries are often regarded as "insipid" in flavor. Thus they go largely unpicked and uncultivated, dropping when they are ripe and staining driveways, patios, and cars with their purple juice, to the annoyance of many people.

Mulberries, however, can be much more than a summertime irritation. With the aid of seasonings such as cinnamon, cloves, nutmeg, mace, or lemon juice, you can coax them into being quite enjoyable. At the same time, you can benefit from their vitamin content and the fact that they are usually free for the picking.

To obtain them easily, simply place a plastic sheet under a convenient mulberry tree, shake its limbs to loosen the berries, and then gather them from the covering below.

Because the mulberry resembles the blackberry without the blackberry's acidity, it can be prepared in the same way. See the blackberry chapter (pages 13 to 30) for more recipes, remembering to use some of the spices mentioned above if they are not already included.

MULBERRY MUFFINS

Here the berries will appear as purple polka dots within the batter.

2¼ cups sifted all-purpose flour
6 tablespoons granulated sugar
3½ teaspoons baking powder
⅛ teaspoon salt
1 teaspoon ground cinnamon
¼ teaspoon ground mace
1 egg, lightly beaten
1 cup milk
1 teaspoon lemon juice
6 tablespoons melted butter
1 cup mulberries

1. Preheat the oven to 425°F. Grease well a muffin tin or tins.
2. Sift together the flour, sugar, baking powder, salt, and spices and set aside.
3. Mix together the egg, milk, lemon juice, and melted butter.
4. Make a well in the center of the dry ingredients and pour in the liquid mixture all at once. Stir to moisten the dry ingredients. The batter will be lumpy.
5. Fold in the mulberries, then spoon the batter into the well-greased muffin tins, filling the cups two-thirds full. Bake in the preheated oven for 12 minutes, or until done.
6. Cool slightly and serve with butter.

Makes 1 dozen.

MISSISSIPPI MULBERRIES

This homey recipe is one of the ways that Anna Lee Howard of Canton, Mississippi, uses mulberries to the delight of those around her, especially her grandchildren. The use of saltine crackers in dough is not uncommon in the rural Deep South.

¼ teaspoon cornstarch
¼ cup water
1½ cups mulberries
¼ cup honey
¼ teaspoon cinnamon
1 tablespoon butter or margarine
1 cup crushed saltine crackers (about 24 crackers)
¼ cup unsifted flour
1 egg yolk
1 tablespoon chicken fat, or 2 tablespoon butter or margarine
3 tablespoons sour milk or water

1. Preheat oven to 350°F.
2. Mix the cornstarch and water. Place the berries in a 1-quart casserole; add the cornstarch mixture, honey, cinnamon, butter or margarine, and mix well.
3. Mix cracker crumbs, flour. Cut in the shortening with a pastry blender or two knives. Add the sour milk or water and egg yolk. Form into a ball.
4. Roll out on a floured board and place over the berry mixture.
5. Bake for 45 minutes. Serve warm.

Serves 4.

SIMPLE BERRY BOMBE

A molded ice cream dessert that makes a spectacular appearance.

Blackberries, blueberries, elderberries, gooseberries, raspberries, or strawberries may be substituted if you wish.

2 pints commercial ice cream, softened
2 cups chopped mulberries

1. Place the softened ice cream in a bowl and stir in the chopped berries until they are well blended.
2. Spoon the mixture into a tall, attractive 4-cup mold whose interior has been slightly moistened with cold water. Freeze for at least 12 hours.
3. Unmold to serve.

Serves 4.

SPICED MULBERRY JAM

4 cups mulberries
3 cups granulated sugar
2 tablespoons lemon juice
1 tablespoon ground cinnamon

1. Prepare the mulberries by stemming them and covering in cold, slightly salted water. Let them stand for 5 minutes, then drain well.
2. Crush the berries slightly, then simmer, uncovered, in a preserving kettle until soft (about five minutes). Add the sugar, lemon juice, and cinnamon and boil until thickened.
3. Skim off the foam; pour into hot, sterilized jars and seal immediately (page 11).

Makes about 1 pint.

HONEYED MULBERRY SHERBET

Blackberries, blueberries, elderberries, gooseberries, raspberries, or strawberries may be substituted in this recipe.

2 large bananas
1½ cups fresh mulberries
1½ cups plain yogurt
¾ cup orange juice
½ cup honey
1 cup canned crushed pineapple, well drained

1. Mash the bananas and mulberries in a blender or by hand. In a large bowl combine the mashed fruit and the remaining ingredients. Mix well.
2. Freeze until firm but not quite solid (about 8 hours). Beat until creamy.
3. Spoon into a 6-cup mold and freeze until very firm (about 12 hours). Unmold and let soften slightly before serving.

Serves 4 to 6.

SNAPPY MULBERRY SAUCE

Pumpkin pie spice livens up the quiet taste of mulberries. Pour this over cake, ice cream, French toast, or waffles.

2 cups mulberries
½ cup light corn syrup
2 teaspoons cornstarch
1 tablespoon cold water
½ teaspoon pumpkin pie spice
2 tablespoons fresh lemon juice

1. Place the berries and the corn syrup in a saucepan. Blend the cornstarch and the water, and then stir it into the mulberry mixture. Stir in the pumpkin pie spice.
2. Bring to a boil over medium heat, stirring continually. Boil, uncovered, for 1 minute. Remove from the heat and stir in the lemon juice.
3. Serve warm.

Makes 2 cups.

BERRY-GO-ROUND

As berries appear in season, pluck them off the vine so they can add romance to this extravagantly delicious sauce. Use it as a topping on cake and ice cream and even as a condiment with meat or poultry long after summertime has fled. It is best if you use at least five kinds of fruit and those given below make tasty companions, although other fruits and berries can make fine substitutes. For example, you could use blackberries, blueberries, gooseberries, elderberries, and/or raspberries.

1 pint brandy, rum, or high proof bourbon
1 pint mulberries
1 pint sliced strawberries
1 pint sliced peaches
1 pint pitted sour cherries
1 pint fresh currants
12 cups sugar

1. Add the brandy, rum, or bourbon to a lidded, sterile stone crock. As they become ripe add the various fruits, making sure that all imperfect specimens are discarded. With each pint of fruit add 2 cups of sugar. Stir well after each addition of fruit and sugar.
2. Store the covered crock in a cool, dark place such as a basement. The refrigerator may be used also. After all the fruit has been added, continue to keep the covered crock in its storage place for at least 2 months before using.
3. The sauce can be served from the crock or, if storage is a problem, it can be packed and sealed into jars.

Makes at least 1½ gallons.

MULBERRY UPSIDE-DOWN CAKE

Blackberries, blueberries, currants, and elderberries may be substituted.

Fruit Mixture

2 cups mulberries
¾ cup granulated sugar (more or less to taste)
2 tablespoons flour
2 tablespoons lemon juice
1 teaspoon cinnamon
¼ teaspoon nutmeg

Batter

½ cup (1 stick) butter or margarine
1 cup granulated sugar
3 eggs
2 cups sifted all-purpose flour
1 tablespoon baking powder
¼ teaspoon salt
¾ cup milk
1½ cups chopped nuts
Grated rind of 1 orange

1. Preheat the oven to 350°F. Grease a 10 x 10 x 2-inch cake pan.
2. Combine berries, sugar, flour, lemon juice, cinnamon and nutmeg. Spread on the bottom of the pan.
3. To prepare the batter, cream the butter or margarine and gradually beat in the sugar. Add the eggs one at a time, beating well after each addition.
4. Sift the flour, baking powder, and salt. Alternately add the dry ingredients and the milk to the butter or margarine mixture, beginning and ending with the dry ingredients. Fold in nuts and rind.
5. Pour the batter over the berry mixture and bake for 45 minutes or until the cake tests done. Loosen the edges and invert onto a serving platter while hot. Serve warm.

Makes about 10 servings.

RASP-BERRIES

"Be off," says the Fairy,
"As quick as you can,
Over the meadows
To the little green lane
That dips to the hayfields
Of Farmer Grimes:
I've berried those hedges
A score of times;"

—From "Berries"
by WALTER DE LA MARE

While gnomes and fairies are fond of berries of all kinds, there is evidence to suggest that they regard the raspberry as the most desirable of all for feasts and merrymaking of many kinds. They are well able to understand the delicacy of the raspberry, and its semisweet, wild flavor is reminiscent of the very lives that they themselves live in the woods. Choice red raspberries, for example, are selected for their rubylike appearance, stuffed with chopped nuts and hummingbird's egg, and served at one of the grandest celebrations in the calendar of the fairy year.

Human beings enjoy raspberries, too, but often must pay dearly for them. Because of their delicacy they easily fall apart when handled roughly or quickly, so a carton of whole raspberries in the supermarket is apt to be highly priced. Still, such a purchase comes only a few times a year, and the taste of fresh raspberries, covered faintly with that soft furriness, may be well worth its price.

Raspberries are available all year long in frozen packages at supermarkets, with and without sugar added.

One 10-ounce package of frozen raspberries = 1 cup (½ cup syrup, ½ cup raspberries)

You're in luck if you live near a raspberry patch, and well you may because raspberries grow plentifully throughout the eastern and midwestern states. Picking them may make you feel somewhat like a jewel thief, for ripened raspberries on bushes resemble nothing less than rubies. When ripe they pull away easily from the vine, leaving no stem at all. You can wash them just before you are ready to use them, but do so quite carefully. They are very fragile.

To freeze raspberries, see the general directions on pages 8 and 9.

We usually think of raspberries as being a deep red, but they can be black, too, and these are often sweeter than their ruby cousins and sometimes called "black caps." A relative of the raspberry is the wineberry, which grows wild along parts of the East Coast. Not wine-colored at all, the wineberry is a reddish orange and may be prepared like the raspberry.

RASPBERRY-CHAMPAGNE SOUP

4½ cups raspberries
½ cup granulated sugar, or to taste
1 cup orange juice
½ bottle champagne
2 tablespoons Cognac or sherry
Fresh mint leaves

1. Puree 4 cups of the raspberries in a blender or press them through a sieve. Add the sugar, orange juice, and champagne. Chill well.
2. Just before serving, add the Cognac or sherry. Garnish with the remaining berries and fresh mint leaves.

Serves 4 to 6.

RASPBERRY-CARROT SLAW

¼ cup mayonnaise
¼ teaspoon celery seed
1 teaspoon lime juice
1 teaspoon grated lime peel
3 cups grated carrots
¾ cup raspberries

1. Mix the mayonnaise, celery seed, and lime juice and peel. Add to the carrots and refrigerate.
2. Gently fold in the raspberries just before serving.

Serves 4.

CHICKEN BREASTS IN RASPBERRY SAUCE

An elegant dish that gives raspberries the starring role in a main course.

4 to 6 whole chicken breasts
¼ cup (½ stick) butter
Salt to taste
⅓ cup raspberry jam
½ cup white port
⅓ cup chicken stock or broth
Grated rind of ½ orange
Grated rind of ½ lemon
1½ tablespoons honey
¼ teaspoon celery seed
1 pint raspberries

1. Preheat the oven to 350°F.
2. Place the chicken breasts in a baking pan and cover them with dollops of butter. Season them lightly with salt and let bake, uncovered, for 1 hour or until lightly browned and crisp.
3. While the chicken is in the oven, prepare a sauce by combining all of the rest of the ingredients except the raspberries. Let simmer, uncovered, in a saucepan until the jam melts.
4. Turn the oven temperature down to 325° F. Pour the sauce over the chicken breasts and continue baking until the meat is done, about 15 minutes. Baste frequently with the sauce.
5. Remove the chicken from the oven and pour the sauce into a separate saucepan. Skim off the fat from the top and add the raspberries. Heat through until the berries are warm.
6. Place the chicken breasts on a warm platter and serve the sauce separately.

Serves 4 to 6.

THREE WAYS TO SERVE FRESH RASPBERRIES

1. Combine raspberries with pineapple chunks. Marinate in a few drops of kirsch and place the mixture in a hollowed pineapple shell.
2. Serve raspberries mixed with a little lemon peel over lime sherbet or sprinkle them on a lime pie for a tart and sophisticated combination of flavors.
3. Shower pear halves, filled with small balls of softened, cinnamon-sprinkled cream cheese, with raspberries.

RASPBERRY-APRICOT MOLD

One 3-ounce package raspberry gelatin
1 cup boiling water
½ cup plus ⅔ cup cold water
1 pint raspberries, chilled
1 package unflavored gelatin
2 tablespoons lemon juice
½ cup heavy cream, whipped, or 1 cup whipped topping
Two 3-ounce packages cream cheese, softened
2 cups drained, diced apricots

1. Dissolve the raspberry gelatin in the boiling water. Stir in the ½ cup cold water. Chill until partially set and then fold in the raspberries.
2. Soften the unflavored gelatin in the ⅔ cup water, then dissolve over hot water. Stir in the lemon juice and cool.
3. Combine the whipped cream and cream cheese. Fold in the unflavored gelatin mixture. Chill until partially set and then fold in the apricots.
4. Turn the apricot mixture into a 6-cup swirl mold, then add the raspberry mixture. Stir slightly with a knife. Chill overnight.

Serves 8 to 10.

RASPBERRY-PEANUT BUTTER FREEZE

1½ cups graham-cracker crumbs
¼ cup (½ stick) melted butter or margarine
¼ cup granulated sugar
One 9-ounce container whipped topping
½ cup milk
One 10-ounce package frozen raspberries, thawed and drained, with liquid reserved
½ cup peanut butter
2 teaspoons cornstarch
1½ teaspoons lemon juice

1. Mix the crumbs, butter or margarine, and sugar and press half of the mixture into a 10 x 6-inch baking dish. Freeze until firm, about 30 minutes.
2. Mix the whipped topping with the milk. Blend in the raspberries and peanut butter. Spread over the firm crumb mixture and then sprinkle the rest of the crumbs over the raspberry mixture. Return to the freezer for 1½ hours.
3. Combine the reserved raspberry liquid with the cornstarch and lemon juice. Cook over medium heat, stirring until thickened.
4. Remove the dessert from freezer 5 minutes before serving and serve with the slightly cooled syrup.

Serves 6 *to* 8.

RASPBERRY MOUSSE

1 quart raspberries
½ cup dry white wine
½ cup granulated sugar
2 envelopes unflavored gelatin
½ cup cold water
½ cup boiling water
1 cup heavy cream, whipped

1. Place the berries in a blender and blend until they are almost smooth. Sieve to remove seeds. (Or simply sieve them without using blender.) Place them in a bowl with the white wine and sugar. Mix well and chill.
2. In a small bowl, sprinkle the gelatin over the cold water. Let stand for 1 minute. Add the boiling water and stir until the gelatin is dissolved. Let the mixture stand to cool.
3. Add the gelatin mixture to the berries. Beat with a wire whisk or rotary beater until fluffy. Fold in the whipped cream and blend well.
4. Pour into a 2-quart oiled mold and chill until set.
5. Unmold to serve.

Serves 6 to 8.

PEACH MELBA

This classic combination of raspberries and peaches was named in honor of Australian-born Nellie Melba, who dazzled audiences throughout the world with her operatic soprano voice. Melba toast was named after her, too, and she herself, originally named Helen Porter Mitchell, took the stage name "Melba" to honor the city of Melbourne, Australia.

2 cups raspberries
½ cup apple jelly
Granulated sugar to taste
1 teaspoon cornstarch
1 tablespoon cold water
4 peach halves, well drained
Ground cinnamon
4 scoops vanilla ice cream

1. Strain the raspberries to remove their seeds. Place the juice in a saucepan, add the apple jelly, and bring the mixture to the boiling point. Add sugar to taste, then thicken with the combined cornstarch and cold water, mixing well. Boil 1 minute, stirring the mixture constantly.
2. Sprinkle each peach half with cinnamon and fill with a scoop of ice cream.
3. Drizzle the hot raspberry sauce over the ice cream and serve the sundaes immediately.

Serves 4.

REGAL RASPBERRY-NUT CAKE

Cake

3 cups sifted all-purpose flour
1½ cups granulated sugar
3 teaspoons baking powder
½ teaspoon salt
1 teaspoon ground cinnamon
¼ teaspoon freshly grated nutmeg
¾ cup (1½ sticks) butter or margarine, softened
⅓ cup milk
2 teaspoons vanilla extract
½ cup fresh or frozen raspberries (if using fresh, sprinkle with 1 tablespoon sugar and let stand until juices run)
1 cup plus 2 to 3 tablespoons chopped nuts

Glaze

1½ cups confectioners' sugar
1 tablespoon butter, softened
2 to 3 tablespoons reserved raspberry juice
Milk, if needed

1. Preheat the oven to 350°F. Generously grease and flour a 12-cup tube pan. Set aside.
2. Combine all the cake ingredients except the raspberries and nuts. Beat for 3 minutes at medium speed.
3. Stir in the raspberries, which have been well drained (reserve the juice for the glaze), as well as 1 cup of the chopped nuts. Spoon into the prepared pan and bake for 45 to 60 minutes, or until the cake tests done.
4. Cool upright in the pan for 30 minutes, then invert onto a serving plate. Let cool completely before drizzling with a glaze made by blending all the glaze ingredients, including a few drops of milk, if necessary.
5. Sprinkle the remaining 2 to 3 tablespoons of nuts over the glaze.

Serves 10 to 12.

RASPBERRY ROLY-POLY

Blackberries, blueberries, and strawberries (sliced) may be substituted in this recipe.

Cake

4 eggs
½ teaspoon salt
¾ teaspoon baking powder
¾ cup granulated sugar
1 teaspoon almond extract
¾ cup sifted cake flour
Confectioners' sugar

Berry Filling

1 pint raspberries
3 tablespoons sugar
2 tablespoons kirsch
One 8-ounce package cream cheese, softened
Confectioners' sugar as needed

1. Preheat the oven to 400°F. Grease a jelly-roll pan; then line it with greased wax paper.
2. Beat together the eggs, salt, and baking powder until thick and lemon colored. Gradually beat in the sugar and almond extract. Fold in the cake flour.
3. Turn the batter into the prepared jelly-roll pan and bake in the preheated oven for 10 minutes, or until the cake springs back when touched lightly.
4. Turn the cake immediately onto a clean towel that has been lightly dusted with confectioners' sugar. From one of its shorter sides, roll the cake in the towel rather tightly. Place on a wire rack to cool.
5. Sprinkle the berries with the granulated sugar and liqueur. Press the berries ever so slightly, then let stand for 20 minutes.
6. Beat the cream cheese until soft. Gradually beat in the liquid that the berries have produced, then fold in the berries. Add confectioners' sugar to sweeten and stiffen the mixture; the amount will depend on how much juice has come from the berries.
7. Set aside ½ cup of the filling. Unroll the cake and spread the remaining filling inside; roll again tightly. Place seam side down on a serving platter.
8. Spread the rest of the filling on the top of the roly-poly and slice to serve.

Serves 8.

RASPBERRY TORTE

"Heaven on a plate" is what Carol Makielski's friends call this lovely dish, topped with berries freshly grown on Makielski's Berry Farm in Ypsilanti, Michigan. The crust is crunchy, the filling rich, and the raspberries tart for an intriguing trio of flavors.

Crust

2 cups sifted all-purpose flour
½ cup packed brown sugar
1 cup (2 sticks) butter or margarine, softened
1 cup chopped walnuts
5 or 6 tablespoons water

Filling

One 3-ounce package cream cheese, softened
1 cup confectioners' sugar
1 tablespoon vanilla extract
1 cup heavy cream, whipped, or 2 cups whipped topping

Raspberry Topping

1 cup granulated sugar
3 tablespoons cornstarch
1½ cups raspberry juice
1½ quarts raspberries

1. Preheat the oven to 400°F.
2. To make the crust, sift together the flour and the brown sugar, mixing well. Cut in the butter with a pastry blender or two knives. Mix in the nuts. Add the water and bring the mixture together in a ball.
3. Pat the dough into a 9 x 13-inch baking pan and bake in the preheated oven for 15 minutes.
4. Crumble the crust into pieces while still warm—you can use a fork—then press back down into the pan. Let cool thoroughly.
5. To make the filling, combine the cream cheese, sugar, and vanilla. Fold in the whipped cream. Pour over the cooled crust and refrigerate until the mixture begins to set.
6. For the topping, combine the sugar and the cornstarch and add the raspberry juice. Heat until the mixture boils, stirring all the while. Add the berries. Spoon the entire raspberry mixture over the cream filling.

7. Refrigerate and serve when thoroughly chilled.

Serves 10 to 12.

Note: To make raspberry juice, heat 1½ quarts of raspberries with 1½ tablespoons of water in an uncovered saucepan until they are soft. Strain through a jelly bag or several layers of cheesecloth.

RASPBERRY MERINGUE TARTS

Blackberries, blueberries, and strawberries may be substituted for the raspberries in this airy dessert.

4 egg whites
½ teaspoon vinegar
1 teaspoon vanilla extract
1 cup granulated sugar
½ cup quick-cooking oats
1 cup heavy cream, whipped, or 2 cups whipped topping
1½ teaspoons orange juice
2 cups raspberries, sweetened

1. Preheat the oven to 275°F. Spread unglazed paper on a baking sheet.
2. Begin beating the egg whites. Add the vinegar and vanilla as the mixture becomes frothy. When the egg whites become foamy, gradually add the sugar and continue beating until stiff peaks form. Fold in the oats lightly.
3. Make 8 mounds of meringue on the paper-covered baking sheet, using a spoon to hollow out the centers and build up the sides in the form of shells. Bake for 45 minutes, or until done (they will be dry and very lightly browned). Let cool briefly and then turn onto a serving tray. Cool thoroughly before filling.
4. Combine the whipped cream and orange juice, then fold in berries. Divide equally among the cooled meringues, mounding the filling attractively.

Makes 8 large tarts or about 20 small ones.

FINNISH TWO-BERRY TART

Crust

½ cup all-purpose flour
1½ cups rolled oats
¼ cup sour cream
⅛ teaspoon salt
1 egg, beaten
¼ pound (1 stick) butter, melted

Filling

1 pint raspberries
½ pint blueberries
1 tablespoon potato starch
2 to 3 tablespoons sugar

1. Mix together the flour and the oats. Add the sour cream, salt, egg, and melted butter. Chill to stiffen.
2. Preheat the oven to 400°F. Grease a 9-inch square cake pan.
3. Pat the dough into the cake pan. Bake for 15 minutes; cool.
4. Turn down the oven temperature to 350°F.
5. Mix the berries with the starch until they are well coated. Pour into the baked crust and sprinkle with the sugar.
6. Bake for 15 to 20 minutes or until the berries are soft. Serve warm.

Makes 9 servings.

RASPBERRY-APRICOT JAM

4 cups pitted, diced fresh apricots
1 cup raspberries
2 tablespoons lemon juice
One 1¾-ounce package powdered fruit pectin
7 cups granulated sugar

1. Combine the apricots, raspberries, and lemon juice in a preserving kettle and mash slightly. Stir in the pectin.
2. Bring to a full, rolling boil, stirring constantly. Stir in sugar. Boil hard, uncovered, for 1 minute.
3. Remove from the heat; skim off the foam. Stir and skim for 5 minutes, then pour into hot, clean jars and seal (page 11).

Makes 4 pints.

RASPBERRY AND TART CHERRY JAM

Leola Wasem of Wasem's Fruit Farm in Milan, Michigan, sells her own baked goods and preserves every Wednesday and Saturday morning at the Ann Arbor Farmer's Market. Here is one of her customers' favorites.

1½ pounds red raspberries
1 pound tart pie cherries, pitted
2 tablespoons lemon juice
One 1¾-ounce box powdered fruit pectin
6 cups sugar

1. Combine the fruits and lemon juice in a preserving kettle and stir in the pectin. Bring to a hard boil, uncovered.
2. Remove from the heat and add all of the sugar at once, stirring well.
3. Heat again and bring to a hard boil. Let boil, uncovered, for 1 minute.
4. Remove from heat, skim off foam, and stir well. Pour into sterilized jars and seal (see page 11).

Makes 3½ pints.

RASPBERRY SYRUP

3 pounds granulated sugar
3 cups water
1½ pounds raspberries
¾ teaspoon vanilla extract

1. Boil the sugar and water, uncovered, for 15 to 20 minutes, until it just begins to thicken. Add the berries and boil gently until thickening occurs. Add the vanilla.
2. Strain the mixture through cheesecloth or a jelly bag (page 11). Cool, bottle, and seal. Store in a cool place, away from direct sunlight.

Makes about 1 quart.

TANGY RASPBERRY-ORANGE SYRUP

Serve raspberries atop waffles or pancakes and then add this delicious hot syrup.

One 10-ounce package frozen raspberries, thawed and drained, with liquid reserved
¼ cup granulated sugar
1 tablespoon cornstarch
½ cup orange juice
2 teaspoons grated orange peel

1. Combine the liquid from the frozen raspberries with the sugar, cornstarch, orange juice, and orange peel. Cook over medium heat, stirring all the while, until thickened. Remove from the heat.
2. Stir in the berries and serve warm.

Makes 1⅔ cups.

RASPBERRY RHINE PUNCH

1 quart raspberries
2 cups confectioners' sugar
½ cup water
Juice of 1 lime
3 quart bottles Rhine wine, well chilled

1. Place the berries in a punch bowl. Cover with the sugar, water, and lime juice. Toss lightly to mix. Let stand in the refrigerator, covered, for 8 hours or overnight.
2. Just before serving, add the cold wine.

Fills 40 punch cups.

RASPBERRY RAINBOW REFRESHER

Swirls of orange, ruby, and green combine to create a rainbow effect.

One 10-ounce package frozen raspberries, thawed
Crushed ice
½ cup lime juice
½ cup orange juice

1. Strain the juice from the raspberries.
2. Fill four 10-ounce glasses with ice. To each glass alternately add equal amounts of each of the fruit juices, first raspberry, then lime, then orange. Pour very slowly to obtain intriguing layers of colors.
3. Garnish each drink with the raspberries and serve with straws.

Serves 4.

STRAW-BERRIES

There were never strawberries
like the ones we had
that sultry afternoon
sitting on the step
of the open french window
facing each other
your knees held in mine
the blue plates in our lap
the strawberries glistening
in the hot sunlight

—From "Strawberries" By EDWIN MORGAN,
Published by the Edinburgh University Press

Why is the strawberry, the glamor queen of all berries, named after so humble a substance as straw? It could be because farmers in days of old carried strawberries to market on sticks of straw. Or they may have come by their name from the straw that was put down to cover the soil in which they grew. Nobody knows for sure. But this much is certain: the lovely strawberry has triumphed over its plain Jane name to become the most widely grown and sought after of all berries in the world.

The recipes herein call for washed, drained, and hulled strawberries, with the exception of California Strawberry Dip, in which the caps are used for dipping. To freeze fresh strawberries, follow the general directions on pages 8 and 9.

Strawberries, of course, come in a great many packaged varieties, both canned and frozen, in the supermarket.

One 20-ounce bag of frozen strawberries = about 1 quart (4 cups) whole strawberries

One 10-ounce bag frozen strawberries = 1¼ cups strawberries with syrup

One 17-ounce can strawberries = 1¾ cups berries with syrup

One 21-ounce can strawberry pie filling = 2 cups berries in thick sauce

When you are blessed with a bounty of fresh strawberries, plan to use them within 2 days. If you wait any longer they'll turn soggy and lose their flavor. Simply store them, covered, in your refrigerator.

The beauty of the strawberry is not only skin deep. It is a rich source of vitamin C and is so tasty that it can be enjoyed in its natural, uncooked state. Many of the recipes in this chapter call for strawberries in just that way, adorned only by cream or liqueur. It seems that strawberries beg to be eaten quite simply, which may be one reason why England's William Butler stated, "Doubtless God could have made a better berry, but doubtless God never did."

If you are tempted to bake strawberries, proceed cautiously. Sliced strawberries in cake batter look appealing before going into the oven, but once baked they usually take on an unappealing reddish-brown color and become soggy and textureless, as experiments in my kitchen have sadly shown.

Lacking the tough outer skins of blueberries and cranberries, strawberries can normally be cooked in a short period of time. This makes strawberry cuisine surprisingly simple. And because of their beauty, strawberries make appealing fresh decorations and garnishes for just about any dish you care to mention.

STRAWBERRY-WINE SOUP

1 quart strawberries
1 cup granulated sugar, or to taste
1 tablespoon all-purpose flour
1 cup dry red wine
1 cup orange juice
2 cups water
1½ cups sour cream

1. Slice the strawberries and reserve a few to float on top of the soup.
2. Combine the berries with water in a large saucepan and let simmer, uncovered, for 10 minutes. Put this mixture through a sieve or puree in a blender; return to the saucepan.
3. Combine the sugar and flour. Stir in the wine and orange juice, 2 cups water, and the sour cream. Add to the pureed berries and bring to a gradual boil, stirring all the while. Let boil for 2 minutes.
4. Chill until very cold and serve in soup bowls, adding a few of the reserved strawberry slices to each one.

Serves 6 to 8.

POLISH STRAWBERRY SOUP

If all of your ingredients have been well chilled, you can serve this *zupa* immediately.

1 quart strawberries
½ cup sugar
2 cups cold water
2 egg yolks, well beaten
¾ cup sour cream

1. Rub the berries, with the sugar, through a sieve or whirl in a blender.
2. Mix with the water and add the egg yolks and sour cream. Stir well.
3. Serve well chilled.

Serves 6 to 8.

Note: See the recipe for Nut Dumplings, page 15.

SAN FRANCISCO STRAWBERRY SCRAMBLE

8 eggs
¼ cup light or heavy cream
1 tablespoon orange juice
1 teaspoon granulated sugar
Salt
Freshly ground black pepper
2½ tablespoons butter
1 cup sliced strawberries
¼ cup avocado chunks

1. Beat the eggs with the cream and orange juice. Stir in the sugar and salt and pepper to taste.
2. Melt the butter in a skillet and scramble the eggs. Just before they are done, add the strawberries and avocado chunks. Scramble until set.

Serves 4.

OPEN-FACED STRAWBERRY SANDWICHES

Blackberries, blueberries, or raspberries may be substituted.

One 8-ounce package cream cheese, softened
½ teaspoon grated lemon rind
½ cup chopped nuts
1 cup strawberries, well drained and chopped into small pieces
Brown bread or whole wheat crackers

1. Combine the cream cheese and lemon rind. Blend in the nuts and berries.
2. Spread the mixture on top of small pieces of bread, cut into rounds or squares, or on crackers. This can also be enjoyed between two pieces of bread with lettuce.

Makes 1¾cups.

STRAWBERRY CREPES

Blackberries, blueberries, or raspberries may be substituted here.

Crêpe Batter

¾ cup all-purpose flour
3 eggs
1 cup milk
2 tablespoons fruit-flavored liqueur
1 tablespoon granulated sugar
6 tablespoons melted butter

Filling

One 8-ounce package cream cheese, softened
1¼ cups confectioners' sugar
1 teaspoon almond extract
Grated peel of 1 lemon
½ cup heavy cream, whipped, or 1 cup whipped topping
4 cups sliced strawberries

Garnish

12 large, perfect strawberries, left whole or decoratively sliced

1. In a blender, whirl until smooth all the ingredients for the crêpe batter except the butter. Add 2 tablespoons of the melted butter and blend again. (If you don't have a blender, you can simply mix this by hand, but you'll have to stir constantly after each addition.) If the batter is still lumpy, let it stand for 2 hours before using.
2. Over medium heat brush a 7-inch skillet with 1 teaspoon butter. Each crêpe will take 3 tablespoons of batter, which you can distribute by quickly tilting the pan in all directions. Pour in the batter, let cook until brown on the bottom, and remove the crêpe from the pan.
3. Stack the crêpes in layers as you finish them. (If you are not going to use them right away, stack them between wax paper, wrap airtight in heavy foil, and refrigerate or freeze them until ready for use. They will keep from 2 to 3 days in the refrigerator or up to 3 months in the freezer.)
4. For the filling, beat the cream cheese with the sugar and almond ex-

tract, then fold in the lemon peel and whipped cream. For each crêpe, simply add ⅓ cup of the filling to ⅓ cup of the strawberries; fill, cooked side up, and roll.

5. Lightly brown each filled crêpe in butter on its uncooked side, then garnish each with a large, beautiful berry, a whole one or one that has been decoratively sliced. No more topping than this is necessary for this perfectly rich and sumptuous dish.

Makes about 12 crêpes.

TRIPLE TREAT DELIGHT

Salad

Two 3-ounce packages strawberry gelatin
2 cups boiling water
Two 10-ounce packages frozen strawberries, sliced
One 13½-ounce can crushed pineapple, well drained
2 large bananas, peeled and finely diced
2 tablespoons lemon juice

Dressing

1 cup sour cream
1 teaspoon granulated sugar
¼ teaspoon ground ginger

1. Dissolve the gelatin in boiling water. Add the berries and stir until they thaw.
2. Mix in the pineapple, diced banana, and lemon juice. Pour into a 6½-cup mold and chill for 5 to 6 hours.
3. Combine the sour cream, sugar, and ginger and serve as a dressing over the molded salad.

Serves 8.

AVOCADO-STRAWBERRY RING

Fresh strawberries do something special to this molded green salad.

One 3-ounce package lime gelatin
¼ teaspoon salt
1 cup boiling water
¾ cup cold water
1 tablespoon lemon juice
3 tablespoons mayonnaise
1 avocado, peeled and mashed
1 pint strawberries

1. Dissolve the gelatin and salt in the boiling water. Add the cold water and lemon juice, then chill until slightly thickened.
2. Stir in the mayonnaise and avocado, blending well. Pour into a 3- to 4-cup ring mold and chill until firm.
3. Unmold and heap the center with the strawberries.

Serves 4.

PARISIAN STRAWBERRY SALAD

2 oranges, peeled and sectioned
2 bananas, peeled and sliced
2 pears, peeled and sliced
1 small pineapple, cut in half and sectioned
1 cup strawberries
3 to 4 tablespoons granulated sugar
¾ cup dry white wine
2 to 4 tablespoons Cointreau

1. Place all the fruit in a bowl and sprinkle with sugar and moisten with the wine. Toss gently and refrigerate for at least 2 hours before serving.
2. Remove from the refrigerator and add the Cointreau, tossing the fruit gently. Serve cold but not chilly for maximum flavor.

Serves 4 to 6.

RUBY LEMON RING

A great big beautiful dish that will do you proud at pot lucks and at picnics.

Three 3-ounce packages strawberry gelatin
5⅓ cups boiling water
Two 10-ounce packages frozen strawberries
Three 3-ounce packages lemon gelatin
Two 8-ounce packages cream cheese, softened
⅔ cup mayonnaise
Yellow food coloring (optional)

1. Dissolve the strawberry gelatin in 2⅓ cups of the boiling water. Add the frozen berries and stir until the gelatin becomes thickened and the strawberries thaw. Pour into a 12-cup ring mold. Let chill until firm.
2. Dissolve the lemon gelatin in the remaining 3 cups boiling water; chill until thickened but not firm. In another bowl, beat the cream cheese until it is fluffy. Add the mayonnaise and blend well.
3. Beat the thickened lemon gelatin until light and foamy, then add the cream cheese-mayonnaise mixture and a few drops of yellow food coloring, if you wish.
4. Pour over the firm strawberry mixture. Chill until well set.

Serves 12 to 14.

ROSES AND RUBIES

1 pint strawberries
1 pint raspberries
1 cup confectioners' sugar
¼ cup kirsch, or to taste
½ cup heavy cream

1. Mix all the ingredients well.
2. Chill. Serve in champagne glasses for a special touch.

Serves 4 to 6.

STRAWBERRIES AU NATUREL

Raspberries may be substituted.

1 quart strawberries
⅔ cup plus 6 tablespoons sour cream
⅓ cup plus 2 tablespoons light brown sugar, firmly packed

1. Slice the berries into a large bowl.
2. Add the ⅔ cup sour cream and the ⅓ cup sugar; mix gently.
3. Place in 6 serving dishes. Top each helping with 1 tablespoon sour cream and 1 teaspoon sugar.
4. Chill at least 1 hour before serving to allow the flavors to mix.

Serves 6.

STRAWBERRY-MELON SURPRISE

The surprise comes from the unexpectedly scarlet filling, which is hidden inside the melon.

Raspberries may be substituted.

1 large, sweet melon, such as a cantaloupe or a honeydew
1 quart strawberries
Sugar to taste
½ cup shredded coconut
¼ cup kirsch or Cointreau
Crushed ice
Mint leaves for garnish

1. Cut off the top of the melon. Remove the seeds and strings; scoop the melon flesh into balls.
2. Combine the melon balls with the berries and mix well, adding sugar to taste, coconut, and the kirsch or Cointreau.
3. Fill the melon with the fruit mixture and replace the top. Refrigerate until ready to serve, then place on a bed of ice and garnish with mint leaves.

Serves 4 to 6.

CALIFORNIA STRAWBERRY DIP

1 pint perfect strawberries
1 cup brown sugar
1 cup confectioners' sugar
1 cup granulated white sugar
1 cup sour cream

1. Wash and drain but do not hull the strawberries. Dry them and place them on a platter or in a glass bowl.
2. Arrange the sugars and sour cream in small, separate bowls near the berries.
3. Have the guests use the strawberry greens as handles to dip the berries, coating them first with sour cream and then with one of the sugars.

Serves 3 to 4.

MOLDED STRAWBERRY RHUBARB

These two fruits combine deliciously in all types of ways. Here they team up in gelatin.

One 10-ounce package frozen rhubarb, cut up
1 quart strawberries, mashed
½ cup water
½ cup granulated sugar
Two 3-ounce packages strawberry gelatin
Lettuce and mayonnaise for garnish

1. Cook the first four ingredients slowly until they are soft and well blended. Measure and add *hot* water as necessary to make 4 cups.
2. Add the gelatin. Pour into individual molds or a loaf pan and chill until firm.
3. Unmold or cut into slices. Serve on lettuce, topped with a dollop of mayonnaise.

Serves 4 to 6.

CLASSIC STRAWBERRIES ROMANOFF

Raspberries may be substituted.

1 cup confectioners' sugar
1 quart strawberries
½ cup heavy cream
1 teaspoon almond extract
2 tablespoons orange liqueur or orange juice

1. Sprinkle the sugar over the berries in a medium bowl and toss. Refrigerate for 1 hour, stirring occasionally.
2. Whip the cream until stiff. Add the almond extract and liqueur or orange juice and fold in the strawberries.
3. Serve immediately.

Serves 4.

STRAWBERRIES ROMANOFF MARGUERITE

Raspberries may be substituted.

2 quarts strawberries
2 tablespoons granulated sugar
1 pint strawberry ice cream, slightly softened
½ cup sour cream
2 tablespoons orange liqueur, or to taste

1. Sprinkle the berries with the sugar and chill for 1 hour.
2. Mix together the slightly softened ice cream, sour cream, and liqueur. Fold into the berries.
3. Serve immediately.

Serves 6 to 8.

SWEET SCARLET AMBROSIA

¼ cup shredded coconut
2 pieces very thinly sliced candied ginger or ¾ teaspoon ground ginger
4 cups fresh, sliced strawberries
¼ cup honey
¼ cup Cognac or fruit-flavored liqueur
¼ cup lemon juice

1. Add the coconut and candied ginger pieces to the berries. (You may substitute ground ginger and add it to the dressing, if you wish.)
2. Make a dressing by combining the honey, Cognac, and lemon juice. Add to the strawberries and chill for 1 hour.

Serves 4 to 6.

FLAMING STRAWBERRIES

2½ tablespoons butter or margarine
¼ cup granulated sugar
¼ cup orange juice
2½ teaspoons grated orange rind
¼ cup brandy, kirsch, or Cointreau
1 quart strawberries

1. Melt the butter or margarine in the blazer pan of a chafing dish over a direct, high flame. Add the sugar, orange juice and rind, and 2 tablespoons of the brandy, kirsch, or Cointreau and cook until the liquid begins to bubble.
2. Fold in the strawberries and heat until they are warmed through. Warm the remaining liqueur in a ladle held close to the hot strawberry mixture. Pour over the berries and ignite.
3. When the flame dies, ladle the mixture over ice cream or cake.

Makes 3½ cups.

SHERRY BERRIES

3 to 4 pints strawberries, sliced
1 cup sugar
6 egg yolks
1 cup cream sherry
½ cup heavy cream, whipped, or 1 cup whipped topping

1. Toss the berries with ¼ cup of the sugar and allow them to "bleed" for 2 hours.
2. In the top of a double boiler, beat the yolks until thick and lemon colored. Add the rest of the sugar slowly, beating continually. Stir in the sherry and cook the mixture over simmering water, stirring until it thickens. Remove from the heat and cool.
3. To serve, fold the whipped cream or whipped topping into the yolk mixture. Finally, fold in the berries and pour into glass dessert dishes.

Serves 4 to 6.

CHOCOLATE-RUM FONDUE

Bathe your berries in chocolate for an unbeatable combination of flavors.

2 tablespoons honey
½ cup heavy cream
One 9-ounce bar of milk chocolate, broken into fine pieces
¼ cup finely chopped nuts
2 tablespoons rum
½ teaspoon rum extract
4 cups perfect strawberries, washed and hulled

1. Heat the honey and cream in a fondue pot over a direct, high flame.
2. Lower the flame and stir in the chocolate, stirring constantly until melted. Add the nuts, rum, and rum extract.
3. Have your guests spear fresh strawberries and dip them into the fondue mixture.

Makes about 4 servings.

STRAWBERRY SUSPIROS

Suspiros is Portuguese for "sighs," and these delicate little morsels are often served in and about Lisbon. They make delightful garnishes if placed around cake or ice cream, and guests who bite into their snowy cocoons will be surprised to find scarlet strawberries nestling within.

3 egg whites
1½ cups granulated sugar
½ cup water
1 teaspoon grated lemon peel
1 teaspoon lemon juice
⅛ teaspoon salt
About 12 small, firm strawberries

1. Preheat the oven to 450°F. Butter a baking sheet.
2. Beat the egg whites until stiff.
3. Combine the sugar, water, lemon peel, juice, and the salt in a pan. Bring to a boil and cook without stirring until the syrup reaches the soft ball stage (234°F).
4. Pour the syrup slowly into the egg whites, beating constantly. Continue to beat until the meringue has cooled and become very thick.
5. For each suspiro, spoon a heaping tablespoon of the meringe onto the baking sheet; top with a berry and spoon on just enough additional meringue to cover and seal each berry.
6. Bake for 3 minutes or until golden. Cool on a wire rack. Serve within an hour after baking.

Serves about 4.

PINK PRINCESS CAKE

Cake

One 16-ounce package white cake mix
One 3¾-ounce package strawberry pudding mix
3 eggs
1 cup water
1 cup vegetable oil
½ cup sour cream
½ cup chopped nuts

Frosting

2¼ cups cold milk
Two 1.5-ounce packages powdered whipped topping
1½ packages strawberry pudding mix (3¾-ounce size again)

Topping

3 to 4 cups sliced strawberries

1. Preheat the oven to 350°F. Grease and flour a 10-inch tube pan.
2. Blend all the cake ingredients except for the nuts in a large bowl, then beat for 2 minutes at medium speed. Stir in the nuts.
3. Turn the batter into the prepared tube pan and bake in the preheated oven for 40 to 50 minutes or until the cake tests done. Cool for 15 minutes in the pan, then remove from the pan and finish cooling on a cake rack.
4. Split the cooled cake crosswise into 2 layers.
5. Whip all the frosting ingredients until the mixture thickens (about 5 minutes).
6. Spread the frosting ingredients between the cake layers and on the top and sides.
7. Decorate lavishly with the sliced berries.

Serves 10 to 12.

FRESH STRAWBERRY COFFEE CAKE

This is one of the very few recipes that allow for strawberries to be baked deliciously. It's from the kitchen of Doris Rowe of the Glen Rowe Produce Farm in Ypsilanti, Michigan, where acres of fresh, juicy strawberries grow every spring.

Cake

½ cup granulated sugar
1 cup all-purpose flour
½ cup milk
2 teaspoons baking powder
1 egg
2 tablespoons melted butter
1½ cups strawberries, sliced

Topping

½ cup all-purpose flour
½ cup granulated sugar
¼ cup (½ stick) butter, softened
¼ cup chopped nuts

1. Preheat the oven to 375°F. Grease an 8 x 8 x 2-inch pan.
2. Combine all the ingredients for the cake except the strawberries and beat for about 2 minutes, until well blended.
3. Spread the batter in the prepared pan and sprinkle the berries evenly over the batter.
4. Make the topping. Combine the flour and sugar, then cut the butter in with a pastry blender or two knives until the mixture is crumbly. Toss in the nuts.
5. Sprinkle the topping over the strawberries and bake in the preheated oven for 35 to 40 minutes.
6. Serve warm.

Serves 6 to 8.

STARS-AND-STRIPES FOREVER CAKE

Make an edible American flag with strawberries, blueberries, bananas, and cream to serve on the Fourth of July. Children enjoy helping with this.

One 16-ounce package yellow cake mix
One 3¾-ounce package vanilla instant pudding mix
½ cup vegetable oil
1 cup water
4 eggs
½ teaspoon vanilla extract
½ cup heavy cream, whipped
2 tablespoons confectioners' sugar
1 cup blueberries
1 quart strawberries, sliced in half
3 bananas, peeled and sliced
2 tablespoons lemon or orange juice
½ cup apple jelly, melted

1. Preheat the oven to 350°F. Grease and flour a 13 x 9 x 2-inch pan.
2. In a large bowl combine the cake mix, pudding mix, oil, water, eggs, and vanilla. Beat at medium speed for 2 minutes, or until blended.
3. Spoon the batter into the prepared pan and bake in the preheated oven for 40 to 45 minutes, or until cake tests done.
4. Let cool in the pan for 20 minutes, then turn out onto a large platter or a piece of aluminum foil-covered cardboard. Cool thoroughly.
5. Blend the whipped cream with the confectioners' sugar. Spread over the cake.
6. Using a toothpick, draw a square in the upper lefthand corner of the cake. Place the blueberries in even rows to resemble stars.
7. Create stripes by alternating rows of strawberries and bananas. To prevent the bananas from discoloring dip their slices into the lemon or orange juice.
8. Brush the melted jelly onto the fruit. Refrigerate until ready to serve.

Serves 10 to 12.

Note: If you are covering a frosted cake with plastic wrap to store in the refrigerator or to carry, remember to insert several toothpicks in the cake before covering with the plastic wrap. This will prevent the plastic wrap from sticking to the frosting.

TILDA'S STRAWBERRY CHEESECAKE

Tilda is a wonderful German-born cook who constantly delights her friends with a cheesecake that has not only a cookie-like dough, but the slightly rough texture of farmer's cheese.

Blackberries, blueberries, mulberries, or raspberries may be substituted for the topping.

Dough

6 tablespoons (¾ stick) butter or margarine
½ cup granulated sugar
1 egg
1 teaspoon baking powder
2 cups sifted all-purpose flour, approximately

Filling

4 eggs, separated
Two 12-ounce packages moist farmer's cheese
¾ cup granulated sugar
1 teaspoon vanilla extract
1 teaspoon lemon juice
Ground cinnamon

Topping

4 cups strawberries, sliced
½ cup melted apple or currant jelly

1. Preheat the oven to 350°F.
2. Beat together the butter and sugar, then beat in the egg. Mix the baking powder into the first cup of flour and add gradually to the egg mixture. Add the second cup of flour in the same way.
3. Knead the dough for several minutes. Press on the bottom and the sides of a 10-inch springform pan and set aside while you prepare the filling.
4. To make the filling, combine the egg yolks, cheese, sugar, vanilla, and lemon juice.
5. Beat egg whites until stiff.
6. Fold in the egg whites and pour the mixture over the dough in the springform pan. Sprinkle with cinnamon and bake in the preheated oven for 1 hour.
7. Let cool, then loosen the cake from the sides of the pan with a knife.
8. Arrange the berries on top of the cake. Paint them with the jelly.

Serves 8 to 10.

NOSTALGIC STRAWBERRY SHORTCAKE

Think of Sunday-go-to-meeting clothes, rocking chairs on wide front porches, hollyhocks against white picket fences . . . this lovely treat was often served in this setting—with heavy cream, unwhipped.

If you wish, blackberries, blueberries, mulberries, or raspberries may be substituted for strawberries.

1 quart strawberries
Granulated sugar
2 cups sifted all-purpose flour
2 teaspoons double-acting baking powder
¼ teaspoon salt
1 tablespoon granulated sugar
¾ cup milk
Dash of freshly grated nutmeg
¼ cup (½ stick) butter, softened
2 tablespoons melted butter
1 pint heavy cream

1. Preheat the oven to 425°F. Butter lightly a 9-inch springform pan.
2. Toss the strawberries, sliced if they are large, with sugar and let stand for 20 minutes, or until they begin to bleed.
3. Combine the flour, baking powder, salt, sugar, and nutmeg. Cut in the softened butter with a fork and add the milk, a little at a time, until a soft dough forms.
4. Turn onto a floured board and roll out into two equal rounds, both about ½ inch thick.
5. Place one round in the lightly buttered pan. Brush with melted butter and cover with the second round. (You may also make individual rounds with a cookie cutter.) Bake in the preheated oven for 12 minutes, or until golden brown.
6. Let cool in the pan.
7. To serve, heap the berries between the shortcake rounds and also on top. Pass the cream separately.

Serves 6.

STRAWBERRY WREATH

This delicate cream-puff pastry is filled with strawberries and vanilla pudding.

Pastry

½ cup (1 stick) butter or margarine
1 cup water
1 cup all-purpose flour
½ teaspoon salt
4 eggs

Filling

One 3¾-ounce package vanilla pudding
3 to 4 cups sliced strawberries

Glaze

1 cup confectioners' sugar
2 to 3 tablespoons strawberry juice

1. Preheat the oven to 425°F. Grease well a 12-cup tube pan.
2. Melt the butter or margarine with the water in a saucepan. Dump in the flour and salt all at once and stir until the dough separates from the sides of the pan and forms a ball.
3. Beat in the eggs, one at a time, until well blended.
4. Spoon the dough into the prepared tube pan and bake in the preheated oven for 40 to 50 minutes, or until lightly browned.
5. While the pastry is baking, prepare the pudding according to package directions. Let cool.
6. Remove the pastry from the pan as soon as it is done and slice in half crosswise.
7. Spoon the cooled pudding into the bottom half of the "wreath." Cover with sliced strawberries.
8. Place the top of the "wreath" over the berries and drizzle with a glaze made by combining and blending until smooth the confectioners' sugar and strawberry juice.

Serves 10 to 12.

MARGARET'S BREATHTAKING STRAWBERRY PIE

Margaret does everything in a full-hearted and extravagant way, whether she's planning an art project for children or creating something special in her kitchen, as this recipe shows.

2¾ quarts strawberries (that's why it's breathtaking!)
2 cups water
2 cups granulated sugar
¼ cup cornstarch
1 baked 9-inch pie shell (see Pie Crust for Berry Desserts, page 55)

1. Slice the berries and put 2 cups of them in a large saucepan with 1⅔ cups of the water. Simmer, uncovered, for 3 minutes.
2. Blend the sugar, cornstarch, and the remaining ⅓ cup of water. Add to the simmering mixture and bring to a boil for 1 minute, stirring continually. Remove from the heat and cool thoroughly.
3. Pour the mixture over the remaining berries and mix together. Because most of the berries have gone completely uncooked, the results will be fresh and unmushy. Pour this strawberry mountain into the prebaked pie shell.
4. Refrigerate before serving.

Serves 6 to 8.

STRAWBERRY-PECAN PIE

Here is a delicious way in which Doris Rowe uses just some of the berries that grow on the Glen Rowe Produce Farm in Ypsilanti, Michigan.

Meringue Crust

3 egg whites
¼ teaspoon baking powder
1 cup granulated sugar
1 teaspoon vanilla extract
12 soda crackers, finely crushed
½ cup broken pecans

Filling

1 pint fresh strawberries, or one 20-ounce package frozen ones
Granulated sugar
8 ounces miniature marshmallows
1 cup heavy cream, whipped

1. Preheat oven to 325°F. Butter a 9- or 10-inch pie plate.
2. If using fresh berries, mash them and sugar them slightly, allowing them to stand while preparing the crust. Then drain them, reserving the juice. Or thaw and drain the frozen berries, reserving the juice.
3. To make the crust, first beat the egg whites with the baking powder until frothy and soft peaks form.
4. Add the sugar gradually, beating until the whites are stiff and glossy.
5. Add the vanilla extract, then fold in the cracker crumbs and chopped pecans.
6. Spread in the prepared plate, building up the sides to form a shell. Bake in the preheated oven for 30 minutes, then let cool.
7. For the filling, heat ½ cup of the strawberry juice and add the marshmallows. Cook and stir over a low flame until the marshmallows are melted. Chill the mixture until partially set.
8. Fold the whipped cream and strawberries into the marshmallow mixture. Pile into the cooled crust and chill until serving time.

Serves 6 to 8.

STRAWBERRY GELATIN PIE

Carol Makielski of Makielski's Berry Farm in Ypsilanti, Michigan, has a special way with berries. Here the use of gelatin gives this pie a wonderful color, flavor, and set.

4 cups sliced strawberries
1 baked 8- or 9-inch pie shell (see Pie Crust for Berry Desserts, page 55)
¾ cup granulated sugar
2 tablespoons cornstarch
1½ cups water
One 3-ounce package strawberry gelatin

1. Pour the berries into the prebaked pie shell.
2. Combine the sugar, cornstarch, and water in a small saucepan and bring to a boil. Stir until the mixture is thick and clear.
3. Stir in the strawberry gelatin. Cool the mixture slightly and then pour over the berries.
4. Refrigerate until ready to serve.

Serves 6 to 8.

VALENTINE PIE

Scarlet strawberries and snowy meringue combine so elegantly that this makes a fine finish to a celebration of Valentine's Day.

3 egg whites
½ teaspoon vinegar
½ cup plus ⅓ cup granulated sugar
½ teaspoon vanilla extract
1 prebaked 9-inch pie shell (see Pie Crust for Berry Desserts, page 55)
3 cups strawberries
2 tablespoons cornstarch
½ cup water
Red food coloring
½ cup heavy cream, whipped, or 1 cup whipped topping

1. Preheat the oven to 325°F.
2. Beat the egg whites with the vinegar until soft peaks are formed. Gradually add the ½ cup sugar and vanilla and beat until stiff.
3. Spread the meringue on the bottom and sides of the prebaked pie shell and bake in the preheated oven for 12 minutes. Let cool.
4. Mash and sieve 2 cups of the berries, reserving 1 cup of the choicest. In a saucepan blend the remaining ⅓ cup of sugar and the cornstarch. Add the water and strained berries; cook, stirring all the while, until the mixture thickens and comes to a boil. Boil, uncovered, for 2 minutes; then remove from the heat and add several drops of red food coloring so the mixture becomes a vibrant ruby. Cool slightly.
5. Spread the strawberry mixture over the meringue and chill until set.
6. Spread the whipped cream over top of the pie and decorate with the reserved, choice berries.

Serves 6 to 8.

SUZANNE'S STRAWBERRY-RHUBARB PIE

1 cup sliced strawberries
3 cups rhubarb, cut into small chunks
1½ cups granulated sugar
¼ cup all-purpose flour
¼ teaspoon salt
¼ teaspoon freshly grated nutmeg
Pastry for a Two-Crust Pie (page 20)
1 tablespoon butter

1. Combine the strawberries and rhubarb with the sugar, flour, salt, and nutmeg and let stand for 20 minutes.
2. While the mixture is standing, prepare the crust. Divide in half; roll out one half and fit into a 9-inch pie pan.
3. Preheat the oven to 375°F.
4. Spoon the strawberry-rhubarb mixture into the pie shell and dot with the butter.
5. Top with the remaining pastry, rolled out in one piece or cut into lattice strips. (Suzanne uses a lattice top crust so the bright pink fruit peeks through temptingly.) Seal and flute the edges; cut slashes in the center if you have used a whole top crust. Cover the edges of the crust with a 1½-inch strip of aluminum foil to prevent over-browning.
6. Bake in the preheated oven for 40 to 45 minutes.
7. Serve warm, with vanilla ice cream.

Serves 6 to 8.

SUNSHINE JAM

This remarkable recipe lets the sun cook your berries, giving the jam the most vivid, ruby-red appearance you've ever seen! A good summertime activity for children.

Red currants or raspberries may be substituted.

3 pounds perfect strawberries
3 pounds granulated sugar

1. Rinse and drain the fruit.
2. Place the sugar in a kettle and add just enough water to moisten. Bring to a boil slowly, skimming off any impurities that form.
3. Add the fruit and boil for 3 minutes exactly—no more!
4. With a large spoon drop the mixture into shallow pans and put on a table in the bright sun for about 3 days. Place pans of water under the table legs to keep away crawling bugs; cover with cheesecloth or screening to keep flying bugs away. Stir several times a day. Bring inside each night and also to avoid rain.
5. The mixture is ready when it has thickened and will slide slowly from a spoon.
6. Ladle into hot, sterilized half-pint jars and seal (page 11).

Makes about 4 half-pints.

KATRINA'S JAM

1 quart perfect strawberries
5 cups granulated sugar
½ cup lemon juice

1. Place the berries in a large kettle and cover with the sugar. Let stand for 3 hours.
2. Heat the mixture over a low flame and let boil, uncovered, for 8 minutes. Add the lemon juice and boil for 2 minutes more.
3. Cool slightly and skim. Stir the mixture to prevent the berries from coming to the top.
4. Pour into hot, sterilized jars and seal (page 11).

Makes 2 pints.

MINUTE STRAWBERRY MARMALADE

1 quart strawberries
1 cup orange marmalade
2 tablespoons lemon juice

1. Whirl the berries in a blender with the orange marmalade until the mixture is smooth.
2. Pour into a heavy saucepan and add the lemon juice. Bring to a boil, stirring constantly. Cook, uncovered, over medium heat for 15 minutes, stirring occasionally, until the mixture thickens slightly.
3. Pour into hot, sterilized half-pint jars and seal (page 11), or use immediately.

Makes 2 half-pints.

STRAWBERRY-RHUBARB CONSERVE

2½ pounds rhubarb (enough to make 4 cups, cut up)
1 quart strawberries
7 cups granulated sugar

1. Cut the rhubarb, unpeeled, into ½-inch pieces. Combine with berries in a large kettle. Add the sugar.
2. Slowly bring to a boil, stirring occasionally. When the sugar starts to dissolve, begin stirring frequently to prevent sticking. Cook rapidly until thick.
3. Remove from the heat and skim off any foam. Pour into hot, sterilized half-pint jars and seal (page 11).

Makes 8 half-pints.

OVERNIGHT PRESERVES

Use the most beautiful strawberries you can find for perfect preserves. Do not double this recipe as all ingredients are not increased.

1 quart strawberries
5 cups granulated sugar
1 teaspoon lemon juice

1. Combine the berries and sugar in a preserving kettle and bring to a boil. Let boil, uncovered, for 6 minutes.
2. Add the lemon juice and boil for 5 minutes more, then pour into a bowl and let stand overnight. Pour into hot, sterilized pint or half-pint jars and seal (page 11).

Makes 2 pints.

STRAWBERRY SYRUP

Prepare your favorite pancakes and stack them together, placing sliced strawberries in between each layer. Add this syrup for a delicious finishing touch.

1 quart strawberries
1 cup water
About 4 cups granulated sugar

1. Bring the strawberries and water to a boil in a preserving kettle and cook for exactly 10 minutes—no more! Strain through cheesecloth or a jelly bag (page 11), then measure the juice and return it to the kettle.
2. Add 1 cup of sugar to each cup of juice. Cook over low heat, stirring constantly until all the sugar is dissolved and the mixture comes to a boil.
3. Allow to boil for exactly 2 minutes. Skim off the scum with a ladle.
4. Pour the hot syrup into hot, sterilized pint jars and seal (page 11).

Makes 2 pints.

NO-COOK BERRY SAUCE

Berries will make their own sauce if you give them the chance. Serve this over ice cream, pancakes, waffles, or anything else that needs a berry's touch.

You can use strawberries, blackberries, blueberries, currants, elderberries, gooseberries, mulberries, or raspberries.

¼ cup granulated sugar, or to taste
1 pint fresh berries

1. Simply mix the sugar and berries. If using strawberries, slice them first. If using other berries, mash them very slightly to break their outer skins.
2. Let stand for 20 to 30 minutes. The juices will begin to run into the sugar.

Makes 1 pint.

BERRY GINGER BLUSH PUNCH

Raspberries may be substituted.

1 quart strawberries
2 cups confectioners' sugar, or to taste
1 quart cold ginger ale

1. In a blender, puree all the berries until they are smooth. Mix them with the sugar.
2. Freeze this mixture in ice trays until firm.
3. Remove from the trays and place again, in batches, in the blender. Blend on low speed for about 10 seconds, adding the ginger ale gradually.
4. Combine all the batches in a punch bowl and serve immediately.

Fills about 30 punch cups.

SCARLET CHAMPAGNE PUNCH

1 quart ripe strawberries
Granulated sugar
Juice of ½ lemon
1 quart bottle Rhine wine, chilled
Ice cubes or an ice mold
1 quart bottle champagne, chilled
1 pint club soda, chilled

1. Place the berries in a punch bowl and sprinkle lightly with sugar and lemon juice. Pour half the Rhine wine over the berries (rechill the remainder) and let stand for 2 to 3 hours.
2. Just before serving, put ice cubes or an ice mold into the bowl. Add the rest of the rechilled wine. Pour in the cold champagne and club soda.
3. Stir lightly. Make sure everyone gets several strawberries as well as the punch itself.

Fills about 30 punch cups.

STRAWBERRY GOLD

Here's a milkshake to sip slowly on a steamy midsummer's day.

2 cups cold milk
2 cups cold apricot or peach nectar
2 10-ounce packages frozen strawberries, partially thawed
4 scopps vanilla ice cream
Whipped cream, colored with some of the strawberry juice, for garnish

1. Blend all the ingredients except the whipped cream in a blender for 20 seconds on high speed.
2. Serve in tall, cold glasses, topped with the pink whipped cream.

Serves 4.

STRAWBERRY WINE SLUSH

Tastes like a daiquiri. Raspberries may be substituted.

One 6-ounce can frozen limeade concentrate
1⅓ cups sauterne
16 ice cubes, cracked
1 pint strawberries

1. Whirl all the ingredients in a blender until smooth and frothy.
2. Serve immediately.

Makes 5 cups or 10 portions (4 ounces each).

SPARKLING STRAWBERRYADE

A fine way to drink your berries—from the Strawberry Advisory Board of California, where they grow big and bountiful.

1 pint strawberries, sliced
One 6-ounce can frozen pink lemonade concentrate
Chilled club soda
Ice cubes

1. Place the berries and lemonade concentrate in a blender. Whirl smooth.
2. For each drink, pour ½ cup puree into a glass. Add about ¼ cup club soda and ice cubes. Serve immediately.

Serves 4.

Note: Champagne or lemon-lime soda can be substituted for the club soda in this recipe.

FRUIT FESTIVAL PUNCH

2 cups confectioners' sugar
2 cups water
¾ cup fresh lemon juice, chilled
1¼ cups lime juice, chilled
1 cup pineapple or orange juice
1 pint strawberries
¾ cup crushed pineapple
2 bananas, peeled, sliced, and quartered
One 28-ounce bottle club soda
2 cups crushed ice

1. Bring the sugar and water to a boil in a saucepan. Let boil, uncovered, for 5 minutes. Refrigerate for 30 minutes.
2. Add the cold syrup to the fruit juices and cut-up fruits.
3. Just before serving, add the club soda and ice and stir well.

Fills about 36 punch cups.

BERRIES IN ICE

For festive touches, add berries to partially frozen water in ice-cube trays. Let freeze thoroughly and add to tall glasses. Decorate punch bowls by filling metal jello molds with water. Place in the freezer, and when the water is slushy in texture, add berries and freeze thoroughly. Let float, unmolded, on the liquid in the punch bowl.

BERRY RECIPE SUBSTITUTIONS

BLACKBERRIES

Open-Faced Blackberry Sandwiches. *See Open-Faced Strawberry Sandwiches on page 143.*
Blackberry Crepes. *See Strawberry Crepes on page 144.*
Blackberry Blintzes. *See Blueberry Blintzes on page 36.*
Blackberry Fool. *See Gooseberry Fool on page 106.*
Honeyed Blackberry Sherbet. *See Honeyed Mulberry Sherbet on page 122.*
Simple Berry Bombe. *See page 121.*
Blackberry Roly-Poly. *See Raspberry Roly-Poly on page 133.*
Blackberry Cheesecake. *See Tilda's Strawberry Cheesecake on page 157.*
Blackberry Shortcake. *See Nostalgic Strawberry Shortcake on page 158.*
Blackberry Upside-Down Cake. *See Mulberry Upside-Down Cake on page 124.*
Blackberry Glace Pie. *See Blueberry Glace Pie on page 57.*
Blackberry Meringue Tarts. *See Raspberry Meringue Tarts on page 135.*
Berry-Go-Round. *See page 123.*
No-Cook Berry Sauce. *See page 168.*

BLUEBERRIES

Open-Faced Blueberry Sandwiches. *See Open-Faced Strawberry Sandwiches on page 143.*
Blueberry Crepes. *See Strawberry Crepes on page 144.*
Blueberry-Pumpkin Bread. *See Cranberry-Pumpkin Bread on page 71.*
Blueberry Fool. *See Goosebery Fool on page 106.*
Honeyed Blueberry Sherbet. *See Honeyed Mulberry Sherbet on page 122.*
Simple Berry Bombe. *See page 121.*
Blueberry Upside-Down Cake. *See Mulberry Upside-Down Cake on page 124.*
Star-and-Stripes Forever Cake. *See page 156.*
Blueberry Roly-Poly. *See Raspberry Roly-Poly on page 133.*
Blueberry Cheesecake. *See Tilda's Strawberry Cheesecake on page 157.*
Blueberry Shortcake. *See Nostalgic Strawberry Shortcake on page 158.*
Finnish Two-Berry Tart. *See page 136.*
Blueberry Meringue Tarts. *See Raspberry Meringue Tarts on page 135.*
Blueberry Cobbler. *See See Blackberry Cobbler on page 24.*
Blueberry-Cranberry Jam. *See Cranberry-Blueberry Jam on page 119.*
Berry-Go-Round. *See page 123.*
No-Cook Blueberry Sauce. *See page 168.*
Blueberry Syrup. *See Strawberry Syrup on page 167.*

CRANBERRIES

Pilgrim's Casserole. *Follow the recipe on page 38, first chopping the cranberries and rolling them in sugar to reduce their tartness.*
Pineapple-Cranberry Bread. *See Pineapple-Blueberry Bread on page 44.*
Country-Style Cornbread. *See page 46.*

CURRANTS

Currant Upside-Down Cake. *See Mulberry Upside-Down Cake on page 124.*
Sunshine Jam. *See page 165.*
Berry-Go-Round. *See page 123.*

ELDERBERRIES

Honeyed Elderberry Sherbet. *See Honeyed Mulberry Sherbet on page 122.*
Simple Berry Bombe. *See page 121.*
Elderberry Updside-Down Cake. *See Mulberry Upside-Down Cake on page 124.*
Berry-Go-Round. *See page 123.*
No-Cook Berry Sauce. *See page 168.*

GOOSEBERRIES
Honeyed Goosebery Sherbet. *See Honeyed Mulberry Sherbet on page 122.*
Simple Berry Bombe. *See page 121.*
Berry-Go-Round. *See page 123.*
No-Cook Berry Sauce. *See page 168.*

MULBERRIES
Mulberry Cheesecake. *See Tilda's Strawberry Cheesecake on page 157.*
Mulberry Shortcake. *See Nostalgic Strawberry Shortcake on page 158.*
No-Cook Berry Sauce. *See page 168.*

RASPBERRIES
Currant-Raspberry Soup. *See page 94.*
Open-Faced Raspberry Sandwiches. *See Open-Faced Strawberry Sandwiches on page 143.*
Raspberry Blintzes. *See Blueberry Blintzes on page 36.*
Raspberry Crepes. *See Strawberry Crepes on page 144.*
Raspberries au Naturel. *See Strawberries au Naturel on page 148.*
Classic Raspberries Romanoff. *See Classic Strawberries Romanoff on page 150.*
Raspberries Romanoff Marguerite. *See Strawberries Romanoff Marguerite on page 150.*
Raspberry-Melon Surprise. *See Strawberry-Melon Surprise on page 148.*
Raspberry Fool. *See Gooseberry Fool on page 105.*
Roses and Rubies. *See page 147.*
Simple Berry Bombe. *See page 121.*
Honeyed Raspberry Sherbet. *See Honeyed Mulberry Sherbet on page 122.*
Raspberry Cheesecake. *See Tilda's Strawberry Cheesecake on page 157.*
Raspberry Shortcake. *See Nostalgic Strawberry Shortcake on page 158.*
Raspberry Glace Pie. *See Blueberry Glace Pie on page 57.*
Raspberry Cobbler. *See Blackberry Cobbler on page 24.*
Sunshine Jam. *See page 165.*
Berry-Go-Round. *See page 23.*
No-Cook Berry Sauce. *See page 168*
Berry-Ginger Blush Punch. *See page 168.*
Berry Good Breakfast. *See page 29.*
Raspberry Wine Slush. *See Strawberry Wine Slush on page 170.*
Berries on Ice. *See page 171.*
Raspberry Leaf Tea. *See Blackberry Leaf Tea on page 29.*

STRAWBERRIES
Strawberry Omelet. *See Norwegian Blueberry Omelet on page 34.*
Strawberry Blintzes. *See Blueberry Blintzes on page 36.*
Berried Treasure. *See page 46.*
Red, White, and Blueberry Bars. *See page 47.*
Strawberry Mousse. *See Raspberry Mousse on page 130.*
Honeyed Strawberry Sherber. *See Honeyed Mulberry Sherbet on page 122.*
Simple Berry Bombe. *See page 121.*
Strawberry Roly-Poly. *See Raspberry Roly-Poly on page 133.*
Red, White, and Blueberry Pie. *See page 56.*
Strawberry Glace Pie. *See See Blueberry Glace Pie on page 57.*
Strawberry Meringue Tarts. *See Raspberry Meringue Tarts on page 136.*
Berry-Go-Round. *See page 123.*
Berry Good Breakfast. *See page 29.*
Strawberry Leaf Tea. *See Blackberry Leaf Tea on page 29.*

INDEX